Divorce from a narcissist

A JOURNEY THROUGH THE STAGES OF RECOVERY FROM A NARCISSIST AND REDISCOVERING YOUR TRUE SELF

Bethany Key

Copyright - 2020 -

All rights reserved.

The content contained within this book may not be reproduced, duplicated or transmitted without direct written permission from the author or the publisher.

Under no circumstances will any blame or legal responsibility be held against the publisher, or author, for any damages, reparation, or monetary loss due to the information contained within this book. Either directly or indirectly.

Legal Notice:

This book is copyright protected. This book is only for personal use. You cannot amend, distribute, sell, use, quote or paraphrase any part, or the content within this book, without the consent of the author or publisher.

Disclaimer Notice:

Please note the information contained within this document is for educational and entertainment purposes only. All effort has been executed to present accurate, up to date, and reliable, complete information. No warranties of any kind are declared or implied. Readers acknowledge that the author is not engaging in the rendering of legal, financial, medical or professional advice. The content within this book has been derived from various sources. Please consult a licensed professional before attempting any techniques outlined in this book.

By reading this document, the reader agrees that under no circumstances is the author responsible for any losses, direct or indirect, which are incurred as a result of the use of information contained within this document, including, but not limited to, - errors, omissions, or inaccuracies.

TABLE OF CONTENTS

INTRODUCTION	5
CHAPTER - 1 UNDERSTANDING AND DEFINING NARCISSISM	13
CHAPTER - 2 TYPES OF NARCISSISM	21
CHAPTER - 3 WHAT IS NARCISSISTIC ABUSE?	29
CHAPTER - 4 NARCISSISTIC TACTICS	39
CHAPTER - 5 HOW TO PROTECT YOURSELF WHEN DIVORCING A NARCISSIST	47
CHAPTER - 6 THE PATH TO RECOVERY FREEDOM	57
CHAPTER - 7 TACTICS TO HELP YOU DEAL WITH THE DIVORCE	65
CHAPTER - 8 DIVORCE AND YOUR CHILDREN	75
CHAPTER - 9 THE AFTERMATH	81
CHAPTER - 10 THE PATH TO RECOVERY FREEDOM	87
CHAPTER - 11 REDEFINING YOURSELF AFTER ABUSE	97
CHAPTER - 12 DISCOVER YOUR TRUE WORTH	107

TABLE OF CONTENTS

CHAPTER - 13
  WHEN THE HEALING GETS TOUGH — 117

CHAPTER - 14
  HOW TO LEARN TO LIVE AND LOVE AFTER BEING WITH A NARCISSIST — 125

CHAPTER - 15
  TRANSFORMING YOUR FUTURE INTERACTIONS — 135

CONCLUSION — 143

INTRODUCTION

The narcissist needs people to constantly provide them with love and adoration. This supply of energy is what helps them maintain their false ego. One single person is not going to be able to give them all of the attention that they need, so they will include a variety of different people in their toxic lives to find the supply that they feel is required. You must always remember that the people the narcissist chooses are always replaceable, and their roles in the life of the narcissist can change very quickly. Each person that is in the web of the narcissist will constantly be battling to prove their value.

There are a lot of people that feel as if narcissists are drawn to them like magnets. It may not be that narcissists are more drawn to you, but you may be more at holding on to them. For instance, many people that can easily see the negative attributes of a narcissist such as their need to be the center of attention, the constant reassurance they are seeking, or the sensitivity they have to be slighted. When they see these things, they may not recognize them as narcissistic traits, but they are still unfavorable. Due to the fact that these are unfavorable traits, most people will not go any further with the relationship.

People are often disturbed by the types of behaviors that the narcissist displays. They will disengage themselves from the situation because it is easier than trying to deal with someone who is difficult from the very beginning. The people that tend to stick around the narcissist will handle this type of situation in a very different way.

If you are a person that feels like narcissists are constantly drawn to you, you might need to take a look at your standards for relationships and what behaviors you will and will not tolerate.

To understand whether or not your standards are healthy and will keep you protected, you can ask yourself the following questions:

- At any point in time, have you ended a relationship because of selfishness on your partner's behalf?

- Are you able to set clear boundaries and stick to them?
- Do you know what behaviors in a relationship you will tolerate, and which ones are totally unacceptable?
- Do you rationalize staying in a bad relationship because you believe it can get better? Is this because of the way things started out in your relationship?
- Do you allow your partners to devalue you?
- Is making excuses for your partner's bad behavior commonplace?
- Have you put up with mental, physical, or emotional abuse without leaving?

If you do find that these questions relate to you, it is time to sit back and really look over your standards. You need to find strategies that will help weed out people with bad behaviors before they sink their claws into you.

Exiting a relationship because you feel that someone is taking advantage of you or that they have nefarious intent is not wrong. It may seem difficult to weed out the narcissists, but when you give people too many chances, you are simply giving them more time to manipulate and take advantage of you.

There are also a few different personality traits that narcissists will pick up on and try to take advantage of. Certain traits are found to be more useful to narcissists than others. So, if you are extremely empathetic, have a desire to help others, you are willing to try harder than most to make relationships work, or your sense of responsibility is strong, and you are likely the perfect target for a narcissist.

All of these traits fall into the desires of a narcissist. Most people don't try and hide these positive attributes that they hold. Unfortunately, with this, the narcissist is able to pick their target quite easily.

Narcissists also genuinely enjoy taking advantage of truly intelligent people. Everything in their lives is a game, and roping someone into their game that is smart feels like a major win for the narcissist. The high they get from besting an intelligent person is better than many others.

It's unfortunate because many intelligent people end up being taken advantage of without realizing what is going on before it is way too late, and they have suffered at the hands of the narcissist for far too long.

People that have lived through narcissistic abuse will oftentimes question themselves. The narcissist has made them believe that everything they have gotten they have deserved. Even though this is utterly untrue, it is hard to make someone who has suffered from narcissistic abuse realize that none of it is their fault. At the end of the day, pretty much anyone can become the target of a narcissist. The most important thing that you can do is to pay attention to the new partners you are bringing into your life to make sure it does not end with the abuse and toxicity that comes along with a narcissist.

CHAPTER - 1
UNDERSTANDING AND DEFINING NARCISSISM

Narcissism is a character trait in which someone displays a heightened over-confidence due to their admiration of themselves; they can simply do no wrong. This is an exaggerated behavior that breathes and exudes arrogance, pretentiousness, and a deep-rooted ideology of false superiority. "I am special. Everyone else in the world is below me because they are not me." A person who exhibits narcissistic characteristics is often described as being cocky, self-centered, self-absorbed, and rude. They view life as a playground for manipulating emotion, as an untapped market in which to exploit and to bend the truth at will. They can be viewed as "winners," but they are crude people to be involved with due to their self-described perfection. So, too, are they, liars. Their success—in most cases—is because of their total and complete disregard for other people and their feelings. Or rather, narcissists will push past people no matter what those people are feeling. They view other people as obstacles. We are, basically, their next hurdle to get over. They would most likely push us off the edge of a top-floor balcony if it meant that they would get just a little more ahead of everyone else.

Narcissists are the perennial interrupters of conversation. They constantly crave the limelight; they feel as if they deserve everyone's attention at each and every single turn. They want to be seen. They want to be heard. They want to be the leading figure in any small gathering, work circles, friendship circles, and among the large crowds. They are the people who ooze confidence in every moment. They are very charming people and more often than not, they are quite funny, very sarcastic. They are good company in public, but once at home and in their own respective comfort zones, they shed their charming skins for the emotionally deprived, ostentatious colors that they don when returned to their private and intimate places. They use manipulation and excessive, yet believable, lies as a tool to such an extent that narcissists are almost fanatical individuals in regard to their use of such methods.

Narcissists have such a deep self-belief burning within them. But beneath all of that lies a person who has been deeply affected by life. Narcissists are people, though pretty hardcore ones, who have been shaped by past trauma, past experiences, or past abuse, which, in turn, has crafted them into a person with such anxiety that the line between nervousness and abandonment has morphed and blurred into a singularly, individualistic focus that the adulation that they are constantly seeking is due to their inner mental conflicts that were borne from a lonely and possibly unloved childhood. This has made them develop what we could call external spotlighted arrogance. The definition of this is, simply, a spotlight. Some form of an inner spotlight that externalizes itself—or switches on when it feels like it needs to be seen. It burns so bright that it forces people to shift and focus all undivided attention on the narcissist. This trait or behavioral characteristic, if looked at from a psychological perspective, is most common in children below the age of 10. It is that need to stand out from the rest, to get attention, whether that is from your parents, your family, your friends; it's a phase our brains go through during early childhood development that can be best linked to the behavior-type of being boastful or to brag about something. In a narcissist's case, what they are essentially bragging about is themselves.

We all know a narcissist. They could be our mother or our father; they could have been this way for as long as we can remember and have left us, now in adulthood, shattered, confused, exhausted. They could be our brother or our sister; they were always showered with praise, always told that they were the star—they were serial winners and developed an egotism that has become the prospective difficulties in our lives, still affecting us at this very moment. They could be a work colleague or an employee. But what are the roots of narcissism?

Narcissists tend to view themselves quite differently when compared to others, and they often make those around them feel inadequate and devalued. Here's the kicker—a narcissist always wants everything to be about themselves. You might not mind showering a one-year-old infant with all your attention, but you will start to mind when a 35-year-old demands the same level of attention and achieves it at your expense.

Narcissists easily victimize others by just being who they are, and it is unlikely they will ever change. This might seem rather severe, but until you deal with a narcissist, you will not realize how toxic such individuals can be. To understand NPD, you must first understand the way narcissists think about themselves.

Where Does Narcissism Come From?

Narcissism usually develops in early childhood. I have heard people say many times that narcissistic behavior reminds them of a toddler throwing a tantrum. I tend to agree with this statement based on personal experience. It seems the emotional trauma responsible for narcissism occurs around the age of a toddler, hence the narcissist's ability to handle emotions gets stuck at that level of mental development. That explains their dangerous emotional immaturity, doesn't it?

We all get exposed to trauma during the early stages of our development. It's simply inevitable. Trauma can result from something as simple as not being picked up by our parent as a baby or being fed against our will. It could also result from something more severe like our mother leaving us at the kindergarten for the first time, which can cause a long-lasting fear of separation. Our parents fighting and screaming at each other in our presence can leave their imprints on our subconscious mind, too. So, what kind of trauma produces a narcissist?

Growing up with an either overbearing and/or completely neglectful parent can warp a child's mind and cause them to be narcissistic adults later in life. A parent can be overbearing when it comes a child's performance in school and neglectful when it comes to the child's emotional needs.

The trauma of a narcissist is the perceived lack of control. The inability to acknowledge their own emotions makes a narcissist extremely uncomfortable. Admitting one "wrong" thing about themselves would make them feel as though everything is wrong. So, every abusive and manipulative action they take only serves one purpose: to feel in control. The root of their toxic behavior towards you has nothing to with you, it has everything to do with them. If you play close attention to their accusations, you will see that they, in fact, project their behavior, fears, and doubts on you. A narcissist may often lie, yet accuse you of lying all the time, no matter how much proof you present that they are wrong. They may feel as if everyone is out to get them and that they always get the short end of the stick, so they project their subconscious beliefs on you by accusing you of plotting schemes against them every time there is a simple misunderstanding.

You must keep in mind that narcissists never truly learned how to express and process their emotions. Their parents may have been overly protective and proud of them—but only when they fulfilled their parents' expectations. One could try to do some research about the past of the narcissist in question. Though it usually is difficult to get a clear picture. It's very difficult to find the truth about a narcissist, especially when their parents admit to not having been able to handle their child.

In many cases, one or both of their parents may display some narcissistic traits, too. That does not mean, however, that the children of a narcissist are bound to become narcissistic as well.

At the end of the day, it's not up to you to determine why the person that treated you so badly has become who they are today and it also not necessary for your recovery process. However, what is necessary for your recovery process is that you are aware that it's definitely not your fault in any way that they are a narcissist, and with that, you are not responsible for their chronic toxicity.

This can be an environmental cause that can lead to a forced image of perfection later in life. Another aspect is early childhood abuse. One way to deal with abuse is to see yourself as above it, too clean for it. Taking an abusive history into account, narcissism acts as a wall to prevent being hurt further in the future. Despite the several ways the disorder can be environmental, there is also some belief that the trait can in fact be hereditary. With genetics, though, seeing a specific behavioral trait can be difficult. Often, though it may seem genetic, it is moreover the way that parent or grandparent was raised that gives them the condition. This brings up the question of actual genetics. Science has yet to come to a clear conclusion on that though. Studies have not been able to come to a solid conclusion, and with many different conditions, it is hard to see which is environmental and which is genetic.

Majority of the cases of Narcissistic Personality Disorder, though, always point back to the parents who raised the child. Whether it is neglect, abuse, overprotection, rewarding for insignificance, Munchausen, or even the parent giving the child a hypochondriac disorder or a sense that they are superior, the child's behavior is usually created at an early age. With such a deep-seated basis and such a long time for growth, this makes the disorder even harder to overcome later in life. Changing someone's perspective of how they should see the world when they were raised and to see it differently can be a nearly impossible task. This also can cause more behavioral and personality issues. Taking away the one or only, defense someone has constructed in order to deal with trauma can then lead to an exposed and vulnerable feeling that can cause depression and/or anxiety. What happens then is the person goes from being narcissistic to high-risk Avoidant Personality Disorder, agoraphobia, social anxiety, self-harm, and even suicidal, or an intention of hurting others. People using narcissism to cover an abusive or traumatic childhood would have to be approached with the utmost care.

Even if the issues are genetic, there is really no direct way to treat genetics over a learned behavior cycle. Hereditary behavior issues are something a species line has evolved to. Somehow that series of genetics has evolved to see itself as more significant than others. Whether this has to do with the biological mating habits or some kind of protective reaction of the line, it is part of who the person is. Just as someone is likely to have a stronger inclination to be a leader or one who helps people for a living, being someone who sees themselves as above others will already be in their head from early childhood. As with learned behavior, this comes from one or both parents.

CHAPTER - 2
TYPES OF NARCISSISM

There are many shades of narcissists that exist. If you're dealing with one, then you need to know exactly what kind they are. This is the only way you can figure out how to handle yourself, whenever you're forced to have interactions with them.

So let's get into the various kinds of narcissists that exist. There are three kinds of narcissists that you're likely to encounter if you haven't met them already. Under these, there are also subtypes. First, let's look at the main three: the classic narcissist, the vulnerable narcissist, and the malignant narcissist.

The Classic Narcissist

This kind of narcissist is what first springs to most people's minds when they think of a narcissist. They're the exhibitionists. The grandiose ones. The high-functioning narcissists.

The classic narcissist is the guy who's a braggart, always going on and on about their achievements. She's the gal who feels entitled to special treatment, praise, and a statue in her honor, while you're at it. If you're not delicately and consistently placing your lips on their derriere, then you're uninteresting, at best, or in trouble, at worst.

They hate it when the spotlight moves from them to someone else. They hate it when you share the spotlight with them. They're going to crop you out of pictures, because you looked better, or they perceive somehow you've dulled their glory. For the classic narcissist, even though they already feel superior to the rest of the human race, they have an obsessive need to be perceived as important by others.

The Vulnerable Narcissist

This guy is fragile. He's always "the victim." He's also called a closet narcissist. Compensatory. The vulnerable narcissist is—as far as he's concerned—better than everyone else they meet. What's the difference between him and the classic narcissist? He isn't a huge fan of being the center of attention.

This narcissist is a leech, of sorts. She'll attach herself to people others think of as important, or special. No, she's not going to look for special treatment for herself—but what she will do is try to get people to feel bad for her. She'll suck up to you by being extremely generous with the gifts and compliments. This is how she'll get the attention she wants from you, and get her much needed ego boost.

The Malignant Narcissist

This guy is the stuff of nightmares. You may have heard of him referred to as a "toxic narcissist. They're the worst of the lot, being extremely manipulative. They will exploit everyone around them to no end.

The toxic, malignant narcissist is also antisocial. Not unlike sadistic psychopaths, and their sociopath counterparts, they've got quite a mean streak.

For the malignant narcissist, her goal is to control. Complete domination. She will do and say whatever she needs to, to feel all-powerful. She will lie. She will use violence. Nothing is beyond her. The worst part? She has absolutely no regrets. She is not riddled with remorse. She doesn't understand what it's like to feel guilty. She does enjoy watching other people in pain, though.

The malignant narcissist is the worst of the lot because they can be serial killers with no remorse. They're the kind who become dictators ad don't mind wiping off an entire race from the face of the earth.

Now that we have covered the three major types of narcissists, let's get into the subtypes.

- **Overt versus Covert Narcissist**

Overt and covert narcissists both enjoy making others feel like crap, bragging and looking for the chance to put one over you. The difference between both sub-types of narcissists though, is that while the overt narcissist is very obvious about all this, the covert narcissist is less likely to be noticed.

Usually, covert narcissists are heavy on passive aggression. In fact, it's possible for you to engage with a covert narcissist, and not have a single clue that they just manipulated you. They're quite stealthy in their methods. This stealth is just enough to give them plausible deniability if you find out they just played you like an upright bass.

You need to understand that while the classic narcissist is an overt narcissist, and the vulnerable narcissist is a covert narcissist, the malignant narcissist can be either.

- **Somatic versus Cerebral Narcissist**

Under this sub-type of narcissism, we're clarifying what the narcissist thinks is most important about himself, and others around him. True, the narcissist is always about hogging the spotlight, while everyone else remains in the faceless audience, applauding them.

However, the narcissists under this sub-type still want to be around people who complement them nicely or would be an added boost to their carefully, intricately woven persona. In other words, these narcissists like to show you off—as their property. "Look how smart or beautiful this person is! Aren't I awesome for being friends with them? But forget about them though—look at me! Look how good I look! Look at me big, big brain! Plenty of smarts!"

The somatic narcissist is crazy about her body. She wants to look hot, all the time. She's got to look good. She's got to retain her youth. She'd become a vampire if those existed, so she could stay young forever. She hits the gym hard. She loves mirrors—or more to the point, she loves what she sees in the mirror. She's taken with her reflection. Her wallpaper is her own selfie. Always.

On the other hand, the cerebral narcissist knows everything. Everything! As far as they are concerned, they are more intelligent than anyone in the room. For them, it's important people realize how smart they are, how much they've accomplished, and how much power they wield.

These subtypes can apply to any of the malignant, vulnerable, and classic types of narcissists. There are some who argue that cerebral narcissists are only ever vulnerable narcissists and that somatic narcissists are classic narcissists, always.

On the flip side, there are arguments that this sort of thinking is stereotypical. It is argued that the view is held only because the body is an external thing, so it would make sense that the classic narcissist is also a somatic narcissist; and since the mind is an internal, hidden thing, then the cerebral narcissist must be a vulnerable narcissist.

The trouble with these stereotypical deductions is evident when you think of the average hypochondriac. The vulnerable narcissist can also get the attention they need with their bodies—through either feigning or exploiting an illness they have. Also, it's possible to have a classic narcissist who's also a cerebral one, seeking admiration because of all they've learned or achieved academically speaking.

Unique Sub-Types of Narcissists

Besides the sub-types we've already covered, we have a couple more, which studies have discovered and labeled as special. These subtypes are the inverted narcissist and the sadistic narcissist.

- **The Inverted Narcissist**

This narcissist is both covert and vulnerable and, codependent. They get into relationships with other narcissists, so they can feel good about themselves. In fact, if their significant other is not a narcissist, then there's a huge chance they will get absolutely no satisfaction from their relationship. The inverted narcissist is a victim of childhood abandonment.

- **The Sadistic Narcissist**

This sort of narcissist is malignant and has a striking similarity to psychopaths, and sociopaths alike. They love hurting others. They're like demons wearing a human meat suit. All their interactions are only ever about one thing: control. They get off on making others feel like crap by utterly humiliating them. They also have some really out-there sexual kinks.

CHAPTER - 3
WHAT IS NARCISSISTIC ABUSE?

Narcissists may demonstrate traits that allow them to be characterized and understood by psychiatrists, but this does not mean that all narcissists are the same. Some narcissists have a more seductive pattern to their manipulation, while others are especially virulent and vindictive in their behavior. A similar statement can be made about narcissistic abuse. Narcissistic abuse is an umbrella term that refers to a spectrum of abusive practices. People with narcissistic personality behavior may all be involved in the abuse of one type or another, but some are apt to be more dangerous abusers than others.

Narcissistic abuse is a subject worthy of discussion because of the trauma it causes to the victims. Narcissistic abuse generally does not leave a scar or a bruise. This type of abuse can drive a person to a nervous breakdown or suicide. It can render people so depressed and isolated that they are unable to leave the house or maintain employment. Narcissistic abuse is traumatic enough that there are clinicians that specialize in treating it. And much has been written on the subject to provide guidance to those interested in contributing to this effort.

Narcissistic abuse is a difficult quantity to handle and describe because many people do not realize that they are being abused.

Definition of Narcissistic Abuse

Narcissistic abuse can be thought of as any abuse that a narcissistic person commits against another person. That being said, narcissistic abuse historically referred to the manner of emotional abuse that narcissistic parents committed against their children. Today, we think of narcissistic abuse as the spectrum of damaging words and behaviors that are done by people with a narcissistic personality disorder.

This type of abuse is generally emotional abuse, although narcissistic people can become physical if in a rage. Emotional abuse itself refers to the gamut of words and deeds that can be traumatic to the other person. As we have seen, the narcissistic person is prone to belittle, demean, and bully others as a part of establishing the dysfunctional dynamic of the narcissistic relationship.

Types of Narcissistic Abuse

Those readers familiar with the literature on narcissism may be familiar with the terms gaslighting and love-bombing, which describe types of behavior associated with narcissists. In particular is a effective tactic that these individuals engage in, which serves the purpose of weakening and isolating their target. Gaslighting is essentially a specific type of manipulation. Many different types of narcissistic abuse involve manipulation, a behavior the narcissist is particularly adept at.

The most common type of narcissistic abuse is emotional abuse, as the narcissist typically uses the emotions of the target against them. The narcissist is sensitive to the emotional cues that other people send, and they learn how to use those cues against them. Something as simple as an unconscious gesture that you make when you are happy or when you are sad serves as a clue to the manipulator of what you are feeling. In truth, the manipulator does not sincerely care how you feel because they lack empathy. They use these gestures as sources of intelligence that can be used against you either for manipulation or abuse.

In fact, the distinction between manipulation and emotional abuse is not always clear. Many books have been written that attempt to sanitize manipulation, seeing this as a tactic that people can (and often do) use for good. For example, a parent can manipulate their children into doing their schoolwork. A wife can also manipulate her husband into applying for that job he was recommended for. These types of manipulation are regarded by some as "normal" and not harmful. This leads these advocates for manipulation to see it as a form of persuasion rather than an art that is always used for harm.

Emotional abuse can be simply defined as using the feelings of others as a tool to wound them

Emotional abuse frequently happens in narcissistic relationships because the partner of the narcissist is often a sensitive person—an empath—who is particularly sensitive and responsive to emotional cues. The narcissist in the relationship with the empath, therefore, has not only amply information on what they are feeling but plentiful opportunities to wound them.

In spite of the supporters of manipulation, we can think of both emotional abuse and manipulation as types of abuse that occur in narcissistic relationships. Gaslighting, again, is a type of manipulation that is frequently found in these relationships, but because it is so singular, it is often regarded as a separate type of abuse. The term represents the unique ability of the narcissist to exert control over those around him or her, leading them to doubt that they understand the distinction between reality and fantasy.

This is the crux of gaslighting

The ability of the narcissist to cause the target to question their sanity. The narcissist is able to do this because they are masters at constructing a false reality that others believe in. For example, the narcissist can carefully create and spread a damaging lie that other people accept. Even the person the lie is about may begin to accept the lie, which is the goal.

For example, a vindictive or seductive narcissist may tell others that a co-worker, roommate, or associate is having problems at work and is about to lose their job. The narcissist says that this person has been caught violating office policy. This seems benign enough, but it is a powerful lie that it is easy for the target to believe. The target may then begin looking for another job (which might be the goal of the narcissist), they may subconsciously begin performing poorly at work (thus fulfilling the words of the narcissist), or they experience psychological effects like anxiety and paranoia.

Gaslighting can be more vicious

A narcissist may steal things from your desk or move them around, which may cause you confusion and doubt. They may follow you or get others to follow you to make you paranoid. They can engage in a host of activities designed to loosen your grip on reality. This manipulation also serves to isolate you.

Isolation is a result of narcissistic abuse that can be considered another form of abuse

Most people learning about narcissism and its effects for the first time have difficulty understanding just how damaging isolation is. Individuals who are isolated not only experience psychological symptoms like depression and anxiety, they experience physical symptoms due to a release of cortisol and other hormones, and they are at much higher risk of suicide than the general population.

As we have seen, the narcissist isolates their partner because they have a codependent need to keep the partner in the relationship. You, as the partner of the narcissist, serve the important role of enabling and encouraging their distorted, archaic self. In order to maintain this self, they will belittle, bully, and engage in other abusive behaviors. These behaviors serve to isolate you by lowering your self-esteem and making you depressed, but the narcissist also actively attempts to isolate you by discouraging you from interacting with family and friends or planting the notion that these people dislike you and would not want to be around you.

As the reader may gleam, gaslighting is a type of abuse that pervades the other types because the narcissist requires the reality of the target to be distorted. In simplest terms, if you saw the narcissist for who they really were (and yourself for who you really are), you probably would not want to be in a relationship with the narcissist or around them at all. The false reality the narcissist constructs in there, and your life is in itself a form of gaslighting.

Some indications that you may be a victim of gaslighting include:

- Feeling excessive doubts that you cannot control or explain

- Feeling that the narcissist knows more than you do about everything (even about yourself)

- Feeling that your sense of normal has changed

- Feeling excessive paranoia without a clear cause

- Becoming silent and withdrawn
- Feeling hypersensitive and hyper-vigilant in your normal environment

Phases of Abuse

The abuse cycle is divided into six phases: idealize, devalue, discard, destroy, and hoover. The narcissist naturally engages in this cycle in every relationship that they are involved in. This is not limited to romantic relationships. As the reader may already know, the narcissist is willing to discard even the closest blood relative without a passing thought.

The phases of abuse are also related to the phases of the narcissistic relationship. The idealization phase occurs early on in the narcissistic relationship. This phase may also include so-called love-bombing, which is designed to give the target an idealized view of the narcissist and the relationship. This merely sets the stage for abuse by reeling the target in with a fictitious idea of who the narcissist is. The narcissist wants you to trust them and see them as superior. Idealization allows them to do this by establishing the sort of rapport that human beings usually establish with one another, but which the narcissist is doing manipulatively and deceptively.

Indeed, many people have difficulty leaving narcissists because of the idealized images that were established in the idealization phase. Those who are abused by the narcissist and do not leave eventually will be discarded when the narcissist tires of them or no longer needs them. Before the narcissist discards their partner, they devalue them. This is a type of abusive behavior that involves belittling, bullying, and other behaviors that are designed to establish the relationship dynamic the narcissist wants. In reality, the narcissist does not value you and thinks you are less than they are, so they will naturally say things that reflect how they feel. The point, of course, is that the narcissist sometimes abuses intentionally, but other times they do it merely as an extension of the sort of people they are.

Destruction is a vindictive behavior. To return to the phases of narcissistic abuse, recall that the first type of emotional abuse is a type of manipulation that occurs with idealization. This is followed by more overt emotional abuse in the form of the demeaning and belittling remarks and implications the narcissist makes. Even disregarding your wants and needs is a form of abuse. These serve to devalue you.

We mentioned isolation as a phase of abuse, but we did not talk about disconnection. Isolation can be both physical and emotional. You can isolate yourself by remaining at home or in another location where you are removed from others, but you can also be isolated mentally. The narcissist is skillful at causing you to be both physically and emotionally isolated. A result of this isolation is a disconnection. Human beings normally connect with others of their kind, but a disconnected person has difficulty forming bonds with others and suffers all the physical and mental problems that stem from this.

CHAPTER - 4

NARCISSISTIC TACTICS

You can be able to tell if the person you are in a relationship with is a narcissist based on the kind of behavior he/she exhibits throughout the duration of your relationship. Ideally, you want to be able to figure out if your boyfriend, girlfriend, or even an acquaintance has narcissistic tendencies as soon as possible so that you can sever ties with him/her before you are too invested in that relationship. Here are ten things that a narcissist will always do in a relationship.

He Will Try to Charm You

Narcissists can be quite charismatic and charming when they want something from you. If you are in a relationship with one, he will go out of his way to make you feel special in the beginning so that you trust him enough to let your guard down. As long as you are serving the purpose he wants you to serve; the narcissist will give you a lot of attention and make you feel like you are the center of his world. If someone puts you on a pedestal during the early stages of your relationship, you should pay more attention to the way they act, just to see if they are faking it.

He Will Make You Feel Worthless

After you have been hanging out with a narcissist for a while, you will notice that when you have any sort of disagreement or argument, his first instinct is to dismiss you in a way that makes you feel worthless. He will criticize you in the sort of contemptuous tone that will make you feel dehumanized. When you disagree with ordinary people, you always get the feeling that your opinion matters to them, but with a narcissist, that is not the case. All the things about you that the narcissist claimed to like when he was charming you will somehow turn into negative attributes, and the narcissist will portray himself as a "saint" for putting up with those attributes.

He Will Hog Your Conversations

Narcissists are in love with the way people perceive them, so they will take every chance to talk about themselves. Whenever you try to have a conversation, the topic is always going to change, and it will suddenly be about them. It's never a 2-way conversation with a narcissist unless he is trying to manipulate you into thinking he cares about you. You will get to a point where you really struggle to get him to hear your views or to get him to acknowledge your feelings. When you start telling a story about something that happened to you at work, you will never get to the end of it because he is going to start his own story before you are done with yours. If you make comments on certain topics of conversation, your comments will be ignored, dismissed, or even corrected unnecessarily.

He Will Violate Your Boundaries

From very early in the relationship, the narcissist will start showing disregard for your personal boundaries. You will notice that he violates your personal space, and he has no qualms about asking you to do him favors that he has by no means earned. He will borrow your personal items or even money and fail to return it, and when you ask, he is going to say that he didn't know it was such a big deal to you—the point is to make you seem petty for insisting on boundaries that most decent people would consider reasonable.

He Will Break the Rules

The narcissist will break the rules that you set for your relationship, and other social rules, without any compunction. The problem is that sometimes, we are initially attracted to rule-breakers because they seem to be "bad boys" or "rebels," but those traits are in fact tale-tell signs of narcissism. A person who breaks social norms is definitely going to break relationship rules because relationships are essentially social contracts. If someone is trying to charm you, but in your first few interactions, you observe that he cuts lines, tips poorly, disregards traffic rules, etc., you can be certain that you are dealing with a narcissist.

He Will Try to Change You

When you are in a relationship with someone, they are definitely going to change you in a few minor ways (often unintentionally). However, when you are dealing with a narcissist, he is going to make a deliberate and perceptible effort to change you, and more often than not, it won't be for the better. He will try to break you, and he will try to make you more subservient to him.

You will find yourself making concession after concession, until, in the end; any objective observer can tell you that you are under his thumb. He will cause you to lose your sense of identity so that you end up being a mere extension of him. When you get out of that relationship, you will find it difficult to figure out who you are as an individual because he would have spent the entire duration of the relationship defining and redefining you.

He Will Exhibit a Sense of Entitlement

The narcissist will demonstrate a sense of entitlement for the most part of your relationship. At first, he may seem generous and considerate just to draw you in, but after that, you will see his entitlement rear its ugly head. He will be expecting preferential treatment all the time, and he will expect you to make him a priority in your life (even ahead of your own career or your family). There will be a clear disconnect between what he offers and what he expects, and he is going to want to be the center of your universe.

He Will Try to Isolate You

Any narcissist who wants to control you and make you subservient to him understands that you have a support system of friends and family who won't stand by and let him harm you. So, one of the things he will do once he has faked affection and earned some of your trust is he is going to try and isolate you. He will insist that every time you hang out, you shouldn't bring anyone along. He will make up lies to drive a wedge between you and your friends. He will play into the conflicts that exist between you and your family members to make you lean on them a lot less. If you let him get rid of your support system, he will have free reign, and you won't stand a chance against his manipulation.

He Will Express A Lot of Negative Emotions

Narcissists trade on negative emotions because they want to be the center of attention. When you are in a relationship with one, he is going to be upset when you don't do what he wants, when you are slightly critical of him, or when you don't give him the attention he is looking for. He is going to use anger, insincere sadness, and other negative emotions to make you insecure, to get your attention, or to gain a sense of control over you. If someone you are dating throws a tantrum over minor disagreements or when you aren't able to give him attention, it means that he has a fragile ego, which is a clear sign that he could be a narcissist.

He Will Play the Blame Game

This is perhaps the most common indicator that you are in a relationship with a narcissist. He will never admit to any wrongdoing, and he will always find a way of turning everything into your fault. When anything doesn't go according to plan, he will always point out your part in it, even if he too could have done something to change the outcome of the event. He will never take responsibility for anything, and when he takes action to solve a mutual problem that you have, he will always make it clear that you owe him.

CHAPTER - 5

HOW TO PROTECT YOURSELF WHEN DIVORCING A NARCISSIST

Be Firm in Your Decision

Now we're moving on to the practical side. By reaching this stage it's likely that you've decided that you're right in your choice to divorce the narcissist in your life and you're ready to start the process.

That's good news, and you can be assured that it's a decision that will serve you well in years to come. For now, however, it's vital that you understand what is in front of you.

If you're not sure of your choice or if you're wavering, you're more likely to give in to the continued manipulation and demands of the narcissist. As we'll explore as we move through these steps, it's very unlikely that your partner is going to just accept the decision and make life easier. If anything, they're likely to do everything to make it harder, because they will take your choice to divorce them as a serious personal dig, something that they just can't handle. That means, your decision has to be a solid one, to avoid you changing your mind when a little pressure comes your way.

Assess the Situation Carefully

For sure, everyone is a little different and that means your situation might not fit the description we've given completely, but you will see similarities.

That is the whole point of this – to give you peace of mind that you're right, that you're not going crazy, that you don't have to deal with this and that if you want to divorce your partner because you're simply not happy, you're perfectly within your rights to do so.

However, that doesn't mean you should take the decision lightly.

Ending a marriage, any marriage is difficult and you need to be very sure that you're making the right choice for you. Starting divorce proceedings and then stopping them halfway through is not only distressing and upsetting for all involved, but it's also likely to cost you a fair amount of money in legal fees. In addition, starting divorce proceedings and then changing your mind is not sending the right message to your narcissistic partner.

They will take this as a win, that they've controlled you and changed your mind. They might turn on the charm for a while, keeping you right where they want you and making sure that you don't get any ideas about leaving again, but after a while, everything will just go back to the way it was before, if not worse. They now have this episode to throw at you during moments of manipulation.

So, when you decide to start divorcing your partner, you have to be sure that it's what you want and it's the decision you're going to move forwards with, no matter what.

Be rock sure and steady in your choice. It's normal to have moments of worry, but that doesn't mean you should change your mind.

Adopt a Positive Mindset

Use every single part of your being to try and create a positive mindset. It can be hard in the circumstances but you have to try your best and focus on a brighter future. This will help you to overcome the difficulties that can arise when going through any type of divorce.

Divorcing your partner isn't just a case of – I don't want this anymore, it's a long and arduous process of unpicking the reasons why the relationship has failed, going through the necessary legal processes, splitting all belongings and coming to agreements. In the normal run of things, that can be very hard and very emotional, especially when there are still residual feelings in place. However, when you are divorcing a narcissist, it can be harder simply because trying to divide everything and come to agreements is borderline impossible without medical help.

Knowing this means that you're not going to have any nasty surprises. If you need to come up with a positive affirmation to use wherever things get tough, go do. Put into place mechanisms to help you feel positive and uplifted, whether that's heading out for a run whenever you feel like stress is starting to overwhelm you or simply focusing on your own self-care. It's likely to feel odd at first, focusing on yourself, because you've been so used to being denied this basic right for so long. However, go with it and understand that it's your need and you're right to look after yourself.

Move Forwards with Purpose

Once you're sure that you want to go down this route, you've tried your best to be as positive about it as possible, move forwards with purpose. Keep your eyes on the prize, i.e. that brighter future, and push through the hardships that will come your way.

We're not attempting to make this sound harder than it is, but we want you to be prepared for the reality of divorce, not least divorcing a narcissist. Put a plan together and work through it slowly and methodically.

Points to Remember

This part has been the first one in your step by step guide to divorcing a narcissist. It is about being very sure about your decision because without that foundation your future happiness will remain very unsure. Canceling divorce proceedings halfway through is not a good idea, not least for your bank account.

The main points to take from are:

- You need to be sure in your decision before you start divorce proceedings;

- Reading the informational chapters before will help you understand whether or not you really are affected by narcissism;

- Unfortunately, divorcing a narcissist is a long and arduous road and one which is likely to be difficult at some point. Being as positive as possible will allow you to see the process through;

- Once you're sure of your choice, you must move forwards with strength and purpose.

Know What Is In Front Of You

You've made your decision and you're sure divorce is what you want. Now, you need to do your research and know what is in front of you.

Your road throughout this divorce journey will be unique and will vary from person to person. Everyone has different situations and circumstances and that means your specifics will be unique. If you have children together, your divorce is likely to be a little more difficult, compared to someone who doesn't have children.

It's vital that you make a plan in terms of your finances and where you're going to live and be prepared for whatever else may be thrown at you.

We are going to talk about some of the situations that you need to focus on and some of the problems that might come your way. If you don't have children, the process of dividing up your belongings could be very difficult indeed, and if you own a house together, all of that needs to be dealt with.

You also need to know that your narcissist is not likely to behave well throughout this process. The fact you are divorcing them is a real kick in the teeth to them, and they're going to take it extremely personally, viewing it as a stain on their character. They will throw everything at you in order to punish you for this and also to turn everyone's attention back onto them, viewing them as the hero in the story.

Expect the Worst

We've all heard the old 'expect the worst, hope for the best' line and that's what you need to do during a divorce of this kind. You need to realize that your narcissist is not going to play fair or kind. They're going to throw everything at you, they're going to make you look like the bad one and you're going to have to convince everyone around you that you're not the one in the wrong. At least, that's the way it will feel. We are all far more experienced and knowledgeable about narcissism these days and divorce courts have seen countless situations of this kind. That means you can be sure that everything will be fair in the eyes of those who are dealing with it from a legal point of view. However, don't expect fair from your partner.

It's probably against the rule being positive to say this, but you need to think of the worst-case scenario here and try and prepare for it. By doing that, you're not going to be shocked or momentarily dumbfounded by what your narcissist says or does.

Remember, divorcing a narcissist is a serious kick in the teeth to them, so you cannot expect anything positive from them.

Planning Your Finances and Housing

If you share finances at this point, you need to make sure that you have the cash to be independent at the start. Your narcissist could quite possibly cut off access to joint accounts and whilst we don't know for sure that this will happen, it's something to be prepared for.

Ahead of time, start putting money aside for the period of time before the divorce is finalized and settled. If you're working and you have your own money, make sure your partner doesn't have access to it.

You should also look into possible benefits you can apply for if you're going to be struggling financially in the meantime. There are many places you can go to for help and advice and here you'll be able to find out if you're eligible for any financial help and how to apply for it. Find all of this information out before you leave, so you know what you're dealing with and you don't have any unnecessary shocks or surprises.

Of course, it's likely that as a married couple you're sharing a house. If you own the house between you, you have a mortgage then when the divorce is all finalized the house will make up part of the items and assets which are divided between you, however, for now that needs to be put to one side.

CHAPTER - 6

THE PATH TO RECOVERY FREEDOM

One of the things that you have to realize is that a narcissist does not see the need to seek help from a therapist because after all, they think that there is nothing wrong with them. Recovery is for those who have been through abuse. If you have been or are in a relationship with a narcissist, it is high time that you left and sought help from a professional. It is this kind of support that you need to rebuild your self-confidence and bounce back to your self-esteem.

Trust me; you are better than you have ever thought possible. The narcissist might have managed to puncture your self-confidence and even crush your self-esteem, but most importantly you are just a victim. You are not unworthy like they want you to believe. Finding a health professional that has a specialty in trauma recovery will help you journey through the healing process to recovery. If you are not able to leave the relationship, a therapist can also help you to learn the best ways in which you can communicate effectively with your abuser so that you can set boundaries that they will respect and hence, protect you so that they will no longer take advantage of you.

Here are some of the steps that you will have to go through to help you journey through healing to recovery:

Step 1: Cut Contact

Once you have left the relationship, keep it at that! Stop maintaining contact with your abuser. The main reason why you left is that the situation was not working for you. Therefore, there is nothing that will happen that can make things better. The best way to recover from abuse is for you to block all forms of communication.

If you have joint custody of children, you may not be able to wipe this person entirely from your life. It is therefore advisable to create a strict custom contract, according to which you only communicate on matters regarding your children using third-party channels exclusively! Otherwise, ensure that you have set up court orders for all forms of agreements.

Think about the extreme trauma bonding, the gross abuse, and the addiction that you had with the narcissist. Sometimes the best way is for you to accept that the only way you can recover from such damage is to pull away and cut your losses once and for all. Think of abstaining as a way of protecting yourself from hurt. In other words, each time you initiate contact with your abuser, you are handing them the ammunition to blow you off.

Remember that you lived with them and so they know what your weak points are and how they can wound you even more profoundly. It is not until we heal that we will stop forcing ourselves on the narcissist for love or craving them or even justifying to ourselves giving them a second chance. When we completely stop contact, then we can begin to heal.

Step 2: Release That Trauma So That You Begin Functioning Again

If we are going to heal, we have to be willing to reclaim our power. We have to do the exact opposite of what we used to believe; 'I can fix him/her, I will feel better.' Your power belongs inside you. The moment you take your focus away from your abuser then you will be able to channel that power into rebuilding your self-love and paying closer attention to making yourself whole again.

At first, it might seem like understanding who a narcissist is and what they do is essential. But the real truth is that these things cannot heal your internal trauma. What you need to do is to decide to let go of that horrific experience so that you can be at peace. You will begin to rise, get relief, and balance again once you have decided to take your power where it belongs- inside you.

Step 3: Forgive Yourself for What You Have Been Through

When the insecure and wounded parts of us are still in pain, we often are pushed into behaving like children who are damaged. We are often looking for people's approval and especially from our abuser, we hand our abuser the power to treat us as they see fit. And that's the time you will realize that you have given them all your resources: money, time and health. The most unfortunate thing is that while doing that, you end up hurting the people that matter the most in your life… your children, siblings, parents, and friends.

Yes, it might be hard to forgive yourself for this, but you can do that if you want to rebuild your life and everything that you lost to your abuser. By working through your healing process, you will soon find resolution and acceptance. You can move away from lacking self-love and respect to living a life full of truth and responsibility and well-being.

You will realize that, when you forgive yourself, you acknowledge that this was all a learning curve and this is the experience you learned, and hence, you are going to use that to reclaim your life. It is when you release your regrets and self-judgments that you can start setting yourself free to realize greatness in your life irrespective of what stage you are at. This is the point when you will begin to feel hope again, hope that will steer you forward into fulfillment and a life full of purpose.

Step 4: Release Everything and Heal All Your Fears of the Abuser and What They Might Do Next

Do you know what bait to a narcissist is? Anxiety, pain, and distress. These are the things that can perpetuate another cycle of abuse no matter how we tell ourselves that we have separated from them. It is indeed true that abusers can be relentless. In most cases, they do not like being losers. But one thing that you have to understand is that they are not as powerful and impactful as you may have thought them to be.

They need you to fear and go through pain so that they can function. Once you have healed your emotional trauma, they fall apart. Therefore, it is crucial that you become grounded and stoic by not feeding into their drama; this way they will soon wither away along with their power and credibility.

Step 5: Release the Connection to Your Abuser

So many people have likened their freedom from a narcissist to that of exorcism. When we liberate ourselves from the darkness that filled our beings, we are allowing ourselves to detox and let light and life to come in. If that light has to take over the shade, the darkness has to leave so that there is space for something new to come in. In the same manner, it is essential that you release all the parts that were trapped by your abuser so that you can tap into a more supernatural power, the power of pure creativity.

When you disentangle yourself from the narcissist, it is not just about cutting the cord; it is also about releasing all the belief systems that you might have associated yourself with subconsciously. It is only then that you can break free to be a new person and not a target of a narcissist.

Even though it might be tempting to seek revenge on your abuser, this is something that you have to try hard to avoid. Rage has the power of pulling you back into deeper darkness and a game that your abuser is an expert at, in the first place. The best form of revenge is one in which you decide to take back your freedom and render your abuser irrelevant.

And it is likely going to crush their ego, and they will be powerless and at a loss that they cannot even affect you. Often they are in despair when it hits that you are a constant reminder of their extinction. It is at this point that this ends and your soul contracts to allow love and healing in so that you can be whole again.

Step 6: Realize Your Liberation, Truth, and Freedom

Traditionally, we learn that loving ourselves is a very selfish act. However, when it comes to finding liberation and freedom from the hands of our abusers, it is a very critical step that allows us to take in the truth and let it set us free from captivity. Yes, it is something incredibly difficult to do, but it is a necessary step toward achieving liberation.

Society has taught us that we are treated by others the same way we treat them. However, this is a false premise because we get treatment according to the way we treat ourselves. In other words, the measure of love that we get from others is equivalent to that we feel about ourselves.

Therefore, when we open up to healing and recovery, we are opening the doors for others to love us in reality and in more healthy ways than ever before. It is this act that serves as a template by which we teach our children so that they do not carry around subconscious patterns of abuse that were passed to them by our ancestors. This positive modeling only starts when we decide to take responsibility for our happiness and freedom. We slowly become the change that we would wish to see so that we can let go of being someone's victim and stop handing other people our power.

In other words, we take back our lives by doing everything necessary to aid our inner healing irrespective of what the narcissist does or does not do, something that's now irrelevant either way. It is at this point that we can thrive despite what we have been through and what has happened to us.

CHAPTER - 7
TACTICS TO HELP YOU DEAL WITH THE DIVORCE

Isn't this a statement you tell yourself every day!? It plays in your mind like a mantra, the self- affirmation reminding you that going in the right direction will be worth it in the end. It should be so easy- why stay with someone who has no empathy, care, or kindness towards you, and who wants to see you suffer? Yet it is not as easy as it seems, hence why you need to repeat statements such as this.

This is one thing that many people don't tell you when taking the steps to divorce a narcissist. You need mantras or affirmation- like statements to keep you on course, remind you that this really is in your best interests and that it will be worth it in the end. The psychological, mental, and emotional abuse and trauma you have suffered are real, and regardless of how many times you have been gaslighted, or made to appear crazy, in the wrong or losing the plot, you know the truth in the core of your cells. Being with a narcissist is completely detrimental to your health.

A covert narcissist is exactly this – covert; still in the shadows of their own manipulations, delusions, and shady-hurtful character. They are not (yet) in the open or publicly acknowledged, and is this because you have not yet made the decision to allow them to be seen in their true light? Taking a stand and choosing, with your own free will, inner strength and sheer conviction, that you will no longer allow yourself to be abused, victimized or manipulated allow your partner to be seen, and for you to subsequently finally take the steps necessary to be free from their abuse.

Of course, all of this is something you know – so see these words as a reflection of your own psyche and conscious mind telling you exactly how it is. The fact that you are reading this and have chosen, consciously, to align with your true self and leave your narcissistic partner for good implies that you are already well on course. This is confirmation, and you are heading in the right direction! You are strong beyond measure.

Divorcing a Narcissist: Stop Reacting!

Reaction. The reaction is not the same as a response. When you respond to someone or something, you provide space, wisdom, and awareness to connect on a mature and responsible level. Responding allows for authenticity, the calmness of thought, and clarity in communication. Yet, reacting is something completely different.

The key to your narcissistic partner's success is in your reaction. They need people to become emotionally entwined and engaged with their stories. If there is no reaction then there is no exchange- no one is appeasing or empowering them. Power is a great word to be aware of here. The reaction provides a narcissist's empowerment or a more accurately faulty sense of empowerment. Causing pain, hurt, and manipulation to others is not empowerment. Regardless, reacting provides the sustenance that a narcissist needs, so the best way to heal and begin your own journey of empowerment is to stop reacting and start responding.

Things to Be Mindful Of: How You May Be Reacting!

Your partner attempts to provoke a reaction and you allow it. Instead of taking a moment to slow down, be calm inside, and recognize the intentions of causing destruction, chaos, and harm; you play to their manipulations. Thus, a vicious and highly repetitive cycle can begin and continue for hours or even days on end. The key is to detach and not get caught up in their games. It can be easier said than done, however, the tips and techniques for effective response below can really help with this.

'Snide remarks.' Expanding from example 1, at this stage, your partner should know you very well and therefore know your triggers. Snide remarks or specific comments are a very effective way to get a reaction from you and subsequently enable them to continue in their ways.

'Awareness goes where energy flows!' If you don't give your attention, time, or energy to something, how can it perpetuate? The answer is that it can't. The intentions and motivations of your partner require energy and attention, otherwise, they are formless.

Watch out for the signs. Assuming you have been with your partner for a while you will know the signs to when they are going to begin their games. If they are bored or displaying signs of frustration, stimulation, or boredom this is a sure warning that you will soon become their target for their stimulation. A narcissist needs that 'spark' to feed their egocentricity, self-centeredness, and feelings of self-worth. Without it, their illusions start to crumble down and they have no choice but to look within, seek help, and ways to change; which are of course very rare for a narcissist.

If you feel yourself becoming stressed, anxious, nervous, or heated inside, these are sure signs that you are on the verge of a reaction. Unlike in partnerships where narcissism is not present or a key theme, and where most people are allowed a few moments of blowing off steam or showing weakness; in this relationship, you are not provided the patience, compassion or support necessary. This means that even when or if your partner does happen to be in a serene, kind, or non- narcissistic space you may unfortunately spark them with your own reactive behaviors. It is extremely rare for a true narcissist to see you becoming upset or worked up on your own accord and not use it as a chance for drama, or further manipulation.

A Deeper Look into Divorce and Reaction

Divorce is a serious thing. The process inevitably means that you have decided to part ways, restart your life, and take back your individual resources, belongings, and physical necessities. This in itself is a major red flag in a codependent-narcissist relationship! Your partner's entire identity is merged in the reality that he or she can feed off you, use you as their hidden and subtle yet powerful support system, and bounce off your kindness, empathy, and positive attributes. So, once you starting responding this destroys their world. This can only happen when you begin to respond.

How to Manage Conflict

Managing conflict is the same if not similar to learning how to respond. When dealing with someone with deeply buried narcissism, you need to know how to respond appropriately and in a way that doesn't cause further harm to yourself. Once again, you are not responsible for the narcissist's energy. You may have spent years being the most patient, loyal, loving, and understanding or empathetic partner, yet these qualities are all lost on them. Managing conflict during or after the divorce proceedings should not be viewed as any different.

Please do not make the mistake of thinking that now you are finally free, or soon to be free, that your partner will suddenly 'see sense' or have a heartfelt awakening. They will not. A narcissist will always view you as their scapegoat and wall or mirror to project their stuff onto, so now you are taking the correct steps and working towards your own wellbeing and happiness; they do not want to let go or give you up so easily.

The following steps may seem simple or effortlessly implemented, yet they are not! Narcissists will do everything in their power to maintain their illusion of power, and try to keep you entrapped in their games until it really is all over. So, in order to combat this and manage conflict successfully, do stay committed and completely aligned to the following. They are all necessary for your happiness, peace of mind, and success.

I. Patience

The key to your success when going through a divorce or separation is to focus on your own self and personal qualities. The narcissist has spent months, years, or even decades (hopefully not!) unwilling to change, so they are not going to start now. This signifies that the only way to get through this and see your own intentions and goals materialized is to stay centered and focused on yourself. Having patience is the first step.

II. Staying Centered: Personal Boundaries!

Nothing and no one can take away your power, and this is something to keep in mind when separating from a narcissist. Actually, don't just keep it in mind; know it within. You hold great personal power and with strong boundaries, your mental projections can act as a shield to all of your partner's bs.

III. Kindness, Tolerance and Self-Respect

Above anything else, you need to have self-respect. This links with kindness and tolerance, which are both necessary to manage and deal with conflict harmoniously. The self-respect part is the trinity due to the fact that you won't receive much kindness or respect from your partner, unfortunately. However, you should seek to remain kind and tolerant during the process. There is great truth in the validity of the power of the law of attraction. We attract, magnetize, and harmonize to us what we give out, so any energy or intentions we project we will receive. If you are sending out harmful, hurtful, or separation based vibrations- you shall receive more from your partner. In other words, you cannot fight chaos and narcissism with more destruction or ill wishes! Showing kindness and respect, even if in neutral and indifferent civil ways, will allow you to remain sane, clear-headed, and calm; also enabling you to stay as clear as possible from your partner's detrimental motivations.

IV. Being Your Own Best Friend, Lover and Soul mate

To succeed, you need to be your own best friend, lover, and soul mate. You need to practice self-love and show up for yourself (because your narcissistic partner isn't going to). Being your best self for you allows you to be your best self for others. Even if your partner is incapable of rationality or niceness, this commitment to being the best version of you still has a positive effect. Subtle energy and intentions are real and showing up for yourself in a way which states that you are self- loving, self- respecting and not going to tolerate anything less than harmonious and ethical cooperation, means that the situation will flow better than if you didn't commit to these things. Your vibe projects outwards also influencing physical reality and the experiences you attract. How divorce or separation proceedings go can all be changed and shaped by your mindset.

V. Gaining Support

The importance of peer, family, and friendship support cannot be disregarded when divorcing a narcissist. Your ability to manage conflict is largely tied in with the amount of support you receive. It can be both a coping mechanism and an essential aspect of your recovery and conflict resolution. Narcissists thrive off the social support and cooperation of others.

CHAPTER - 8
DIVORCE AND YOUR CHILDREN

Divorce affects kids, period. There is plenty of disagreement on just what those effects are, but few would argue that experiencing the divorce of their parents has no impact on children. Some would argue that children of divorce are doomed to a life of depression, failed relationships, and eventually divorce. Others would argue that even though there may be short-term pain, the divorce of their parents has no significant impact on a child. I don't agree with either extreme.

First of all, we are all responsible for our own actions. While experiencing the divorce of their parents may make it statistically more likely that a person will get divorced themselves, ultimately each one of us has the ability to choose how much we let things from our past affect us. To blame failed relationships on the divorce of your parents is a cop-out.

On the opposite extreme, there are definitely cases where the parents' divorce is in the best interest of the child. This is usually to extract the child from a bad situation such as abuse, addiction, alcoholism, open infidelity, etc. In these cases, the factors contributing to the divorce will likely have a negative impact on the child even though the divorce is necessary for their emotional or physical protection.

A study was conducted recently by Bowling Green State University and Iowa University that underscores the fact that divorce does impact children. In this study, researchers looked at children with half-siblings, specifically situations where adolescents had half-siblings with the same mother but different fathers. The results were enlightening, indicating that "by age 15 teens who have a half-sibling by a different father are roughly 65 percent more likely to have used drugs. This held true even after the results were adjusted for family background, family instability, and socio-economic factors. The results were more pronounced in firstborn children than siblings later in the birth order.

So what does all this mean?

This study offers proof that divorce hurts kids. It also shows that for younger kids, seeing their mother start a new family with someone other than their father hurts even more. Adolescents in this situation are hurting to the point of turning to drugs and sex to ease their pain.

My goal here is not to put a guilt trip on anyone who has remarried and is starting a new family. I would, however, urge you to take special notice of how your adolescent or pre-adolescent children are adjusting to the new blended family.

If you are reading this, you are seeking some help in dealing with your divorce and that puts you way ahead of most people. But, be aware that your kids may need some help too. Get them the help they need to adjust to the new family situation from a pastor, counselor, or other trusted adviser. Doing so will likely prevent them from turning to drugs or sex to deal with the pain if they are struggling to adjust.

If you haven't started a new relationship yet, please consider the impact it will have on your kids before you do. I have heard some family specialists recommend waiting until your kids are out of the house before you even begin dating.

My hope for you is that you will wait until you are healed to begin dating. Then, when you do venture into new relationships, consider your children's feelings as you proceed. Kids are resilient and they can handle a lot. Everything you do to ease their transition from divorce to Mom or Dad dating, to Mom or Dad getting re-married, will only help them. If you see that they are struggling with the adjustment, get them some professional guidance. Help them deal with their emotions before they turn to drugs, alcohol, or sex.

How and What to Tell Kids

- **Tell the Truth**

The best thing you can do is to just tell your kids the truth, but not necessarily the whole truth. For example, if your spouse is having an affair, your children don't need to know all the sordid details, they only need to know that sometimes things happen that you don't want to happen. You also need to adjust what you tell your children based on their age. A child of three has a different level of understanding than a child of seven, and a child of seven has a different level of understanding than a teenager.

Avoid speaking negatively about your ex, especially to the children. He is, and always will be, your child's parent and your child loves him. You need to do everything you can to help your child maintain a healthy relationship with his or her other parent. Some of the best advice I received from the Divorce Care material was that the truth will come out. You don't have to be the one to tell your children what really happened—they will eventually find out on their own.

- **Tell Them It's Not Their Fault!**

Many children will blame themselves for their parents' divorce. This is normal, but it is something that can be minimized if both parents reassure the child that this is something between Mom and Dad and has nothing to do with them. If the child has experienced feelings of abandonment before, as is alluded to in this question, then it can be especially important that she understands it's not her fault. She may be inclined to think there is something wrong with her, and you need to convince her that this is not true.

Answer your child's questions as truthfully as you can without giving in to negativity. This can be difficult, especially with older children. They can sense when there is more to the story and will often probe to find out what you are leaving out. If you are faced with an overly inquisitive child, just reiterate that the divorce was an issue between their parents and some details are private.

One of the greatest sources of fear for children during a divorce is the uncertainty of how life is going to change. Try to give your child as much information as possible about how life will be different after the divorce. As soon as the details are decided, let them know what the living arrangements will be, if they will be changing schools, how often you will see them, etc. The more time they have to adjust to the changes before they actually happen, the better your children will be prepared to handle them.

CHAPTER - 9
THE AFTERMATH

The aftermath of dealing with a narcissist can be truly felt only once you go no contact and have them no longer in your life. The effects of narcissistic abuse are long-lasting and go way beyond the direct contact with the narcissist and even once they are no longer present in your life, the toxic cloud above your head still remains. Gaslighting, drama, lying, isolation, and a series of other manipulation techniques we talked about leave you mentally numb to the point that even dealing with everyday tasks feels like a burden. The consequences of having such individuals in your life are many, as you are affected on all levels of your conscious and unconscious being. In other words, you feel broken and damaged in the mental, physical, emotional, and spiritual planes. In addition, in cases of many survivors, the narcissist also affected their material reality, which resulted in a loss of status, friends, money, or property.

Survivors of narcissistic suffer a wide range of mental health issues as a result of long-term manipulation and devaluing, all of which have roots at the beginning stages of a relationship with a narcissist. Anxiety and paranoia are some of the most common reactions to being mentally and emotionally abused and are all part of a PTSD, post-traumatic stress disorder. Because of the constant distress and chaos survivors have been part of, they experience flashbacks, intense headaches, have trouble sleeping or intense nightmares. The life with a narcissist leaves our brain in a state of shock and extreme confusion, and traumatizes the mind, causing troubles with concentration and agitation. Survivors have trouble communicating and may experience social anxiety and agoraphobia, the fear of open space, and crowded places. The feeling of isolation stemming from the days of a relationship persists and people who dealt with a narcissist feel too vulnerable to expose themselves to the outer world, which is often followed by a state of paranoia and beliefs that people are evil and want to cause us harm. It is like a constant state of fight or flight.

Since gaslighting is one of the most dangerous, if not the most dangerous form of playing with one's mind, many experiences mild to severe realization, where one feels like they and the outer world are somehow separated. Because of the state of shock, the mind activates these two coping mechanisms, which are a normal response to prolonged stress but can be troublesome if not treated. If you feel like you are an actor in your own life, a ghost of your former self who is not able to feel or be present in reality, it is likely that your mind is just trying to protect you until you heal by shutting the reality off. It is possible that to feel this way even during the relationship, starting as early as the devaluation phase, in which case the depersonalization and realization just deepen once they are gone, until you start to heal.

Another very common side-effect of being involved with a narcissist is depression. Survivors feel blue, have no motivation to take care of themselves and life gets to the point where even taking a shower seems like a huge task. Depression can be mild, but unfortunately, can also be fatal, causing thoughts of ending one's life or even suicide. The life and has been drained and the survivor is left in a fog, with no self-esteem, no drive, and no hope for a better future. All energy was given to the narcissist and the relationship that they just can't find the strength to continue with their life, especially if love for the narcissist is still there. You are made to believe there is nothing about you to love. Your dreams and ambitions have been extinguished and you believe you are not lovable unless you are perfect or can fulfill someone's demands. You don't feel good enough, let alone capable of moving on, so who wouldn't feel depressed? Narcissists are like predators who feed off of other people's energy—they take your light and give you their darkness. And they will show absolutely no remorse for what you are going through, but that is okay because you will heal and they will always be stuck their pathological ways.

The effects of narcissistic abuse are such that avoidance feels like an escape. The constant feeling of not knowing what to expect from the narcissist is combined with low self-esteem and a feeling of utter worthlessness. Because of that, survivors feel incompetent and view themselves how a narcissist described them. They see themselves through narcissist's glasses and believe they will be rejected, denied, and discarded everywhere they go, and all of this together causes them a lot of anxiety.

Since the abuse has damaged the core of self, survivors feel like they don't have an identity, as a relationship with a narcissist is a codependent one, and thanks to constant projection, there is no clear line between who is who. When it all ends, many don't know who they are, feel like nothing has meaning anymore, and feel powerless. Anyone who has dealt with a covert knows very well how it feels like not to be allowed to be authentic, to thrive, how it is to feel alone while being in a relationship, to feel guilty for standing up for yourself and putting healthy boundaries. Such a person knows what it is like to be trapped in guilt for things that are not your fault all the time, to be afraid to express oneself, and doubt every decision you make.

Don't feel ashamed if you feel this way. You are not weak, you are completely opposite. Know that you are not alone, even if it feels like it. There are others who, just like you, suffer from the effects of loving a narcissist and they too feel alone. Some survivors find escape in substance abuse, some battle with sexual dysfunction and some develop a physical illness or eating disorder due to constant stress and feeling not good enough or beautiful enough. If any of this resonates, just don't feel down about yourself. Don't blame yourself as it is not your fault. These are all very human and very normal reactions to being exposed to months and years of narcissistic abuse. And most importantly, don't compare yourself to others who are able to live their life to the fullest shortly after a breakup, as a relationship you had was far from normal or healthy.

All of this happens because you suddenly start to realize with whom you have dealt with, and as time goes by, things start making more sense. You start noticing your part in the game, but most importantly, you start seeing the narcissist for who they truly are. However, in the beginning, truth is hard to comprehend and your mind might as well try to protect you from a flood of emotions until you're ready to face it. Unlike the narcissist, you are a healthy individual who was infected with someone else's virus and you can get back on track and you can restore your life. Even if breathing feels like a burden now, one day you will look at your relationship with them and be proud of yourself, because you will win this and you will endure, no matter how impossible it feels at the moment.

CHAPTER - 10
THE PATH TO RECOVERY FREEDOM

Many people will breathe a sigh of relief after the divorce is finalized just to realize that things are not as done as they would like them to be. We are going to take a look at the different things the narcissist may attempt to bring you back into their war zone and the reactions you should have to ensure you shut them down each and every time.

You must also realize that the time it takes to heal from the abuse you suffer when a narcissist can take quite a bit of time. Depending on the severity of the abuse, you may be looking at some serious long-term damage. Understanding that you have been through a traumatic event is the first step toward healing. We will look at a variety of different things you may be facing when it comes to healing and the steps you can take to regain control, self-confidence, and happiness.

Post-Divorce Combat with a Narcissist

Those that divorce narcissists quickly find that life is still difficult even when the court hearings are over. You must never forget that the narcissist has an inane need for attention. They need the focus of the world to be on them. This is completely exhausting and probably at least part of the reason you divorced them. When you were married to the narcissist, you were never enough, and that is not going to change now that you have divorced them.

Once you divorce a narcissist, you must understand that things are not going to simply become peaches and cream. Realistically, there may not be a ton of differences at all, to begin with. You have to remember that while you will be growing, healing, and changing, the narcissist will not. They will not be able to see that they have made mistakes, and they will continue to try and gain your attention at pretty much any cost. They will not be concerned about the consequences.

Finding the strength, power, and drive to reclaim your life is no easy feat. It is something that will have to be worked toward. There are many aftereffects that can play a role, and it can feel like a war zone when it comes to dealing with the narcissist that you just divorced. You will be facing a variety of different challenges.

Let's take a look at some of the things that you may experience after finalizing your divorce with the narcissist in your life.

You may find that you are still in a frequent state of confusion. Narcissists will use things like gaslighting, criticism, lies, and double standards to make you feel crazy and confused. You must remember they love to play these kinds of games so that they have full power and control. Once you are outside of the relationship, the damage that this kind of thing can have on a person is lasting.

You will need to work on rebuilding your self-esteem and your ability to trust your own thoughts, memories, and feelings.

Be aware that the narcissist that you just divorced will still try and continue to play these games with you. They are so used to winning when you are around that they will seek it out. It can be difficult to avoid interaction with your ex. This is especially true when there are children involved.

Having a strategy to deal with many situations where you need to be in contact with your ex is a great start. Don't be afraid to reach out to a friend or family member to join you for face to face conversations with the narcissist. They can help cement what actually happened, which can, in turn, help you learn to trust yourself more.

The manipulation game may have worked on you for a long period of time, but you don't have to let it go on forever.

You should also understand that changing your phone number and possibly the locks on your house can also be a great course of action. Some even find that they need to change the email address and things of that nature. They do this because a narcissist is a person of tenacity. They will likely want to continue to have your attention and will go to great lengths to do it.

Some people that have divorced narcissists end up having issues with the ex, bombarding them with nasty text messages, emails, and other forms of communication.

If you have a volatile narcissistic ex-spouse, you may also want to inform your friends, family, and place of business. You never know what type of slanderous things the narcissist may try to soil your name and reputation. By making the people in your life aware of what is going on, you are taking a proactive approach to keeping the narcissist out of your life forever. Completely cutting ties when you can is the best option.

For those of you who have suffered the abuse of a narcissist for a long amount of time, don't be afraid to ask for help. It can be hard to trust yourself in the early time after leaving a narcissist.

They have spent all of their time wearing you down so that you would have no confidence or conviction in life. It takes time to work through these issues and asking for help to get through daily life can be very helpful in building your confidence and showing yourself that you can, indeed, do it without the narcissist.

More than likely, the narcissist in your life is not going to simply disappear. You can pretty much guarantee it if there are children involved.

While you may not be able to cut ties completely, you will need to set very clear boundaries. The narcissist may ignore them. If they do make sure to jot down what is going on so that if you end up back in court, you have the evidence you need to show the true colors of your ex-spouse.

When you divorce a narcissist, you take away a decent amount of their power, and they hate it. They will use a variety of different tactics to draw you back in so they can continue to use you for their own purposes. By creating chaos, they believe that they will also gain control. This can be some control over you and/or the children that the two of you have. You may find that they ignore orders from the court, or they start making false claims against you. These things are both done to rope you in and ensure that you continue to play the narcissists game.

You can't stop them from doing these types of things, but you can know that they are coming, which can give you time to figure out the best way to handle it when it does.

If there are kids involved, you should also be prepared for your ex to try and use them against you or, even worse, turn them against you. The narcissist can be very charming, and when they want to, they can appear to be a great parent and person. Depending on the age of your children and the experience they have had with the narcissist, the thought of this can be emotionally devastating.

You must know that you cannot control what happens when your kids are with their narcissistic parent; you can only control your own personal reactions and actions.

It may seem like a great idea to fill your children in on who their other parent actually is, but this can actually do more harm than good. Kids are actually pretty smart when it comes to the intent that people hold. They will quickly realize which parent is truly there for them and supporting them in a healthy way and which parent is not. You should not speak poorly of your ex or use your children to spy on what is happening at your ex's house.

Don't stoop to the level of the narcissist and use your children as pawns in a never-ending game of non-sense. Instead, protect them and show them what a healthy relationship between a parent and a child should look like. If they have questions or concerns, be open and honest with them. Answer their questions with kindness and compassion toward the other parent. They will see that you are trying, and all it will do is tighten the bonds between you.

Taking the high road is not always easy; however, it is always going to be the best answer to the question of how to handle the children during and after a divorce.

Realize that they have nothing to do with it and do your very best to keep them out of it. This can be so hard when you are dealing with a narcissist. They do not care enough about anyone to not include them in their nefarious games. Shielding your children, the best you can by providing them with genuine love and support is the best thing you can do when they have to deal with a narcissistic parent. Remember not to take the things your ex says to heart and encourage your kids to think for themselves.

Obviously, every situation is different, and each person's experience with a narcissist can vary. Some of you may be lucky, and the narcissist will move on quickly, leaving you alone to pick up the pieces and take back the control in your life. For those of you that are not so lucky don't give up. Stay strong and focused on healing and starting your life over once the divorce is finalized.

Eventually, they will prey on someone else, and in the meantime, you will continue to build the skills you need to handle them in a way that will not bring harm to yourself or to your children.

Healing From a Narcissistic Marriage

Healing from divorce is not an easy thing. Healing after divorcing a narcissist is even harder. They will go to great lengths to continue to keep control over you. What you once believed about human decency will be unraveled once you have experienced the pain of divorcing a narcissist. Their behavior is completely deplorable and devastating.

One of the reasons that it is more difficult to heal from a divorce with a narcissist as compared to a regular divorce is that being with a narcissist is more like war than it will ever be like love. Most relationships have good memories, and it allows us to get over the loss of the relationship. The memories of a relationship with a narcissist will be memories of feeling helpless, belittled, and crazy. Let's take a look at a few other reasons that healing from a narcissistic relationship is more difficult than recovering from a normal break-up.

HEALING AFTER A DIVORCE FROM A NARCISSIST

One of the biggest hurdles to overcome is accepting the fact that your entire relationship with your ex was one-sided. It was only ever about the narcissist and what they wanted or needed. This is a truth that can be hard to swallow. When you are devoted to someone, you hope and oftentimes expect that they are also devoted to you.

CHAPTER - 11
REDEFINING YOURSELF AFTER ABUSE

Despite the fact that narcissistic abuse can leave behind marks or injuries so deep that you may feel that you will never be able to truly cleanse yourself of them, you can recover from it. Of course, you can never turn back time, and therefore erasing the effect of narcissistic abuse altogether is impossible but you can get yourself back to your healthy self. You can care for yourself and help yourself heal. Even though, in the throes of abuse, you may not be able to recognize the person you see when you look in the mirror, you can get that sense of identity back. You can reclaim it and if you are willing to put in the effort, you will get it back.

It does not matter how long the relationship you were in lasted, nor does it matter how much abuse you endured, you can always hope to heal. While the healing process is not easy by any means, it is possible, and you will be able to do it. This will guide you, step by step, through the process of healing, pointing you in the right direction so you can begin to work on yourself. As you work, you will get to the point where you recognize your smile in the mirror. You will feel peace of mind for the first time in ages. You will feel happier, and maybe even love, again. No matter what the narcissist has told you, you are capable of change and healing, and you absolutely deserve a life filled with happiness and peace. You are worthy of love. You are worthy of respect. You are worthy of loving the person you see looking back at you in the mirror.

Acknowledge Your Abuse

Healing begins with acknowledgment. If you cannot acknowledge that what the narcissist has put you through is abuse, you may not be ready for this process. By recognizing what happened as the abuse it was, you will be able to take the steps necessary to correct for it and heal. You will erase any of the denials you have hidden the abuse behind as long as it occurred by naming it. Naming it abuse releases your blame in the abuse. No one asks for their loved ones to hurt them the way the narcissist may have hurt you, nor does anyone deserve it. When you say that the narcissist abused you, you say that the narcissist made a conscious decision to inflict unwanted harm upon you, and that pushes the blame you may have internalized from yourself onto the narcissist. With that blame lifted, you will be able to begin working on yourself.

As you go through this process, do not forget that you only control yourself. You must be responsible for yourself but you do not control how those around you react. Even if you did something as cruel as punching someone on the street, you are not in control of the other person's reaction. You did not deserve what the narcissist did to you, regardless of how minor or extreme the narcissist's manipulation may seem to you. You were an unfortunate victim, chosen because your own traits made you desirable. Instead of lamenting that some of your traits made you a victim, you should celebrate the ones that attract a narcissist—empathy and compassion are fantastic for people to have. Being patient and seeking peace is an admirable way to live. These are not bad traits to have and they do not make you a lesser person. These are traits of a good person. In this situation, the narcissist took advantage of the good person you are and used your best traits against you. Treat yourself kindly as you consider this and remember that you did not ask for it to happen.

Forgiveness and Compassion for Yourself

With the acknowledgment of the abuse, you can then move on to forgive yourself. As you established, your traits and strengths should be celebrated, not punished. Forgive yourself for blaming yourself for the abuse so you can begin to celebrate those parts of yourself. You will be able to forgive yourself for not seeing the red flags when they happened, reminding yourself that your good nature may have been to see the good in everyone but ultimately the narcissist choosing to take advantage of that is not your fault.

You can forgive yourself for not leaving the relationship sooner, reminding yourself that you tried desperately to care for the narcissist, truly loving who he was, and that love was taken advantage of. Your good heart, your compassion, and kindness when you see someone suffering, were taken advantage of. When you recognize that, you can forgive yourself.

Remember, forgiveness does not necessarily come easy but you deserve to forgive yourself. You did not intend for the situation to get as bad as it did and you are making an effort to heal the best that you can. You did your best in the situation with what you had, and that is enough. Yes, you were in a bad situation for a period of time but you survived. You were strong enough to cope as it happened and you were strong enough to say you are ready to get help and begin healing just by virtue of having opened this and reading as far as you have. That deserves celebrating as you work through healing.

Remind yourself to give yourself the compassion you would show other people. If your friend came to you in this situation, telling you the story you yourself have, how would you react? Would you be supportive? Would you be kind and understanding? Or would you look at her with a cold, hard look, and tell her that she should have tried harder to leave in the beginning? Would you have told her that the abuse was her own fault and that she had been asking for it? The answer is most likely no, you would not. Treat yourself with that same compassion as well. You must forgive yourself and treat yourself kindly if you hope to move on toward healing the rest of you.

Grieve Properly

Despite the fact that your relationship with the narcissist took a turn toward abusive, you still likely developed real, strong feelings for her. You loved her, or rather, the idea of her that she originally presented to you when attempting the love bombing stage, when she mirrored your heart's desires. You fell in love with an idea, which quickly was obliterated by the narcissist that was left behind, staring back at you with the face of the one you loved as if your loved one had suddenly become possessed. You deserve the chance to grieve that relationship. Though the person that you loved was never a real person, she was real to you, and because of that, you should allow yourself to grieve. If not for the person you lost, then grieve for not getting the relationship you deserved when you fell in love with the narcissist.

Grief involves five stages that occur, though they may not happen linearly. Grief also comes and goes and while you may feel better one day, you might suddenly be shocked by feelings of sorrow when you realize that you are once again missing the narcissist. This is normal, and grief is one of those things that never fully goes away; you just learn to live with it.

The first stage of grief is denial. You tell yourself that the relationship does not need to end. You may try to convince yourself that what has happened in your relationship does not warrant breaking up. This is to protect yourself from the pain you will feel when it is officially over. Next, you go through anger. At this stage, you acknowledge the truth in front of you: The narcissist was abusive. At this point, you recognize the narcissist for who she is, and that enrages you. The thought of your abuse, or the abuser that inflicted it, is enough to send you into a fury. Third, you reach bargaining. At this stage, the anger has subsided somewhat, and you tell yourself that there are ways or reasons that the relationship could continue to work. You tell yourself that if you try a little harder, or do a little more, then the abuse would no longer happen. This would be enough to save the relationship, you tell yourself, and you try to grapple with that, even if your bargaining chip ends up being your own wellbeing, such as deciding that you are willing to martyr yourself for the narcissist because you love her. Next, you hit the stage of depression. Here, you acknowledge that the relationship is over. You see that things can never be acceptable, and that dissipates the hope you felt. Lastly, you reach acceptance. At this point, though you may not agree with what happened or that your relationship had to end, you accept the end result and no longer try to fight it.

Release Negative Feelings

As a primary target for a narcissist, you are likely empathetic to some degree. As an empath, you likely have a propensity to absorb the emotions of those around you. You may have internalized some of the narcissist's own negativity because of the exposure to them. You may see some of the narcissist's negative traits in you, such as realizing that you are snapping at people the same way he snapped at you or that you have been thinking about yourself in the way that the narcissist thought of himself. You might feel uncharacteristically angry at the world. No matter the negative feelings, you need to develop an outlet for them.

If left alone, you may feel as though you're very self is festering within you, as though the toxicity from the narcissist still threatens to overwhelm you and turn you into someone you know you are not. The solution to this is to find a good outlet for yourself. Some people pour themselves into a creative hobby, such as drawing, writing, painting, music, dance, or any other form of creating something else. They literally channel their feelings into their art, allowing the negativity to flow through them and out into the world so it can no longer consume them. Others choose physical exercise as an outlet, choosing to sweat out the negativity with each rep of the weight set, or with each mile run. Others still may decide to nurture something else, such as growing and tending to a garden, bringing back those tender feelings that were once familiar to them. No matter what you choose as your healthy outlet, what is important is that you feel better after engaging in it and that you see that your general outlook and mood is improving the more you do it. Anything is acceptable here so long as it allows you to channel your negativity in a way that works for you and that you enjoy.

Find Support Networks

Support networks may be one of the most intimidating parts of healing. Support networks imply that you will be opening up to others about the abuse you endured in person, face to face with others. Some people are not comfortable with this idea but luckily, the internet has made finding groups of people like you easier than ever before.

CHAPTER - 12
DISCOVER YOUR TRUE WORTH

Your self-esteem and self-worth are the value that you placed upon yourself. They are a reflection of whether or not you like yourself. They reflect whether and not you feel that you deserve to be happy and whether or not you show yourself kindness and compassion. They reflect whether or not you are comfortable with your strengths and are aware of the positive things that make you. Your self-worth and self-esteem tell everyone whether or not you believe that you as an individual matter.

Your narcissistic former partner did a number on you so it is understandable if your self-esteem and self-worth are not up to par with what they should be. The first step in rectifying that is becoming more self-aware. You need to have a baseline for what you generally feel about yourself so that you can then use that as a guideline to move forward and increase your self-esteem and self-worth accordingly. Education is your best friend.

Self-esteem and self-worth are not the same things although they might be described as flip sides of the same coin. While your self-esteem is a general gauge for what you think, believe and feel about yourself, your self-worth is recognizing that you can be even greater than these things. High self-worth comes from recognizing that you are lovable, that you are a necessary component to this life, and that your value is beyond measure. In simple terms, self-esteem speaks to you thinking that you are lovable, necessary, and valuable but not necessarily believing this while self-worth is having that absolute conviction of the fact. As a result, having high self-esteem does not equate to having a high sense of self-worth.

Luckily, if you are currently suffering from low self-worth and self-esteem, you are not stuck in this condition forever. There are things that you can do to build your sense of self-worth. Below you will find 5 such measures.

Talk to Yourself Kindly

You may not have realized it but the voice of the narcissist that you lived with for so long may have become your internal voice. Of course, this voice is constantly criticizing you and dismissing your needs as fickle things.

The internal dialogue that goes on in your head is known as self-talk. You may not realize it yet but you have the power to influence what is said because this talk is influenced by your thoughts, ideas, beliefs, and things that you are unsure about. These thoughts, ideas, and others center on your perception of the world around you, other people, and yourself.

This is why self-talk has the power to be both negative and positive. As a result, if you have a negative outlook on life and yourself, your self-talk will predominantly be negative. On the other hand, if you have a more optimistic outlook and personality then this self-talk will be more positive and hopeful.

Self-talk can be influenced by your current level of self-esteem and self-worth. On the other hand, you can increase your sense of self-esteem and self-worth by practicing more positive self-talk.

Even though practicing positive self-talk has so many great benefits, our instinctive human reaction is to practice negative self-talk. This is an evolutionary trait that was used in the time of our ancestors to up the rate of survival. Having a pessimistic view allowed cavemen to better predict the worst-case scenario so that they could be prepared. Even though this practice is not necessary for survival in most cases in modern society, it is still something that persists in the human psyche.

Therefore, to beat this natural human inclination and circumstances that promote it, you must first be aware of what it is and how it happens. Negative self-talk falls into one of four categories. They are:

- Catastrophizing. These types of negative thoughts make the person expect the worst at all times even going so far as to defy logic in the expectation.

- Personalizing. These types of negative thoughts make a person blame themselves for everything that happens even if the circumstances are far out of their reach to control.

- Magnifying. These types of negative thoughts make a person focus on the negative aspects of a situation while blatantly ignoring any and all positives that came out of that situation.

- Polarizing. These types of thoughts take on an either-or approach. Things are only good or bad, or black or white. There is no middle ground and as such, thoughts tend to favor the black or bad.

Now that you are aware of the type of negative thoughts that can persist in your mind, you can then learn to switch them around so that they are more positive. This is a practice that takes a conscious effort on your part to monitor what type of talk goes on in your head.

Let us practice with a few examples.

Your negative thought can be, I have failed and so, will be a failure forever. You can switch that negative self-talk and practice a more positive outlook by instead thinking something like, I am proud of my effort because it took much courage to go outside of my comfort zone.

Another negative thought may take a form like, I am out of shape and should not bother trying to achieve my ideal weight. A positive thought to counter that should be, I am capable and persistent and will do what is necessary to ensure that I become as healthy as can be.

Practicing positive self-talk is another process that does not happen overnight. You have to be persistent and consistent with it to see results. This will allow you to develop a new habit whereby your natural inclination is to take on a positive outlook on the world and yourself. That positive outlook will help boost your sense of self-esteem and self-worth. Tips you can employ to do this include:

- Identifying things that trigger negative self-talk. For example, your work life may be a circumstance where you experience a lot of negative self-talk. Identify what about that situation triggers those thoughts so that you can mentally prepare yourself to counter these thoughts with positive self-talk.

- Stop and evaluate how you feel often. Do this especially when you feel down as this is a time where negative thoughts are likely to manifest.

- Surround yourself with positive people. It is unfortunate to say but you are the company that you keep. Therefore, if you find yourself hanging around people that are perpetually negative then your internal dialogue will take on that energy. Actively choose the type of energy that you absorb and hang out with people who promote positive vibes and interactions.

- Learn to use humor to counter negative self-talk. Humor allows a person to feel lighter and less stressed and therefore, less likely to give in to negative self-talk.

- Use positive affirmations. These statements boost the likelihood that you will take on a more positive outlook and therefore, use positive self-talk to communicate with yourself.

You are now the one in control of your thoughts. Taken even that power away from the narcissist and replace his voice with one the uplifts and empowers you.

Work on Your Self-Image

Your self-image is what you believe about your personality, appearance, and abilities. The narcissist would have taken punches at your self-image as well to suit his purpose of manipulating and controlling you. He would have made you see your physical appearance, your capabilities, and your personality through a lens of his making. This is your wake-up call to look at yourself through a new lens. The best way to cultivate that new lens is to first work on acknowledging the things that you are good at.

Next, if there are things about your personality that you do not like, acknowledge what they are and work on changing them. Personality is a fluid thing. You can change it anytime. You have seen how being in the presence of the narcissist can change your personality for the worst. Now you can work on changing it for the best. One of the surest ways to do this is by changes bad habits that you may have such as being abrasive. Taking on more positive personality traits like being more kind and honest goes a long way in boosting self-image.

One of the hardest-hitting contributing factors for poor self-image is body image. Weight, how we dress, our facial features... All of it and more play a part in how we feel about ourselves. Again, this is something that you can take control of. You need to learn to feel comfortable in your own skin and to see the beauty in you. Beauty is not just skin deep. It is about how you carry yourself, how accepting you are of yourself, and how open you are to the fact that you are a beautiful person. Beauty is not a state of the body. It is a state of mind.

Things you can do to promote a more positive body image include:

- Celebrating and appreciating all the things that your body can do. You can run. You can dance. You can breathe. You exist... All of these things make you special and beautiful no matter how simple or common they are.

- When you need reminding, make a list of the top 10 things that you like about yourself. Read this list often and place it in an area where it is easily visible and accessible to you. This frequent reminder of your likable traits solidifies the facts in your mind and therefore, boosts your sense of self-worth.

- Turn negative self-talk about your body image into positive self-talk.

- Wear clothes that make you feel comfortable and good about your body. Do not try to fit into the social norm. Work with your own body shape, size, and your own needs, not against them to fit in with the current trend.

- Do not allow yourself to be fooled by mass media and social media messages about you what you should be or look like. What you are is beautiful and there is no need to change to fit into a mold.

Be Proud of the Fact That You Are a Survivor of Narcissist Abuse

This narcissist tried to break you but just from reading this I know that you are not broken, merely cracked. A crack can be mended and be transformed into something truly beautiful and inspiring as exampled by you.

Not many people can go through the things that you have gone through and still make it out on top. You are strong and resilient and both of these traits deserve to be celebrated and appreciated, especially by you. Not only have you survived this abuse and taken steps to get out of the vicious cycle, but you have also taken steps to make a bigger, better, brighter future for yourself.

Focus on the change that you would like to make in your life and how you would like to go. As you manifest that change, you will notice the increased positivity in your mental, emotional, and spiritual environment.

CHAPTER - 13

WHEN THE HEALING GETS TOUGH

Healing properly takes time, discipline, and determination. Imagine you broke your arm in several places, so you go to the hospital to get it repaired and instructions on what to do for the pain and to have a fully functioning arm once it heals. In order for this to happen, they have to break your arm again because it has started healing on its own, but improperly. If they do nothing, your arm will mend in a deformed manner, the bones will not be properly aligned. You agree to allow them to break and reset the broken bones so that it can heal properly and be fully functioning once it has completely healed. After the bones have been broken and realigned, you experience a lot of pain, and a cast is placed on your arm to keep it stabilized for several weeks to ensure proper healing.

If the cast is removed prematurely, you run the risk of the bones moving and becoming misaligned and causing it to look abnormal, compromising full mobility of the arm. You agree to the process and keep the cast on, and you keep your arm in a sling throughout the day to ensure proper healing. To function through the pain while the arm is healing, you are given instructions to take pain medication several times a day and instructed to restrict your activities until the cast is removed. After a few months of complying with the doctor's orders, the cast is removed and your arm looks a little thin, but you are able to move it and the pain has subsided.

Just as the physical body has to be nursed and assisted to heal when bones are broken, your eternal body, and your soul—mind, and emotions—has to be nurtured and assisted when you have been wounded or broken emotionally from a failed marriage. You must be guided through the healing process to ensure that you heal properly and are nurtured. Prescribed exercises and instructions are the medication that will help you heal properly. When you are feeling the pain from the wounds and the flood of different emotions associated with your grief, you may become overwhelmed. The assistance I've provided will help you stay on track and continue to heal in a healthy manner. Not working through your emotions properly can delay your healing and cause you to stuff the emotions inside to avoid them. Avoiding the pain and not processing the varying emotions can lead to bitterness, resentment, anger, and depression and can adversely impact your ability to build healthy relationships in the future, as well as impact your ability to return to complete healthy functioning and interaction with others. You may start lashing out at the children or having anger outbursts with the people close to you. If you become depressed and are unable to pull out of it, your daily activities and routines can be adversely impacted.

To stay on track with your journey to wholeness, here are a few things to look for, identify, and push through so that you can stay on course and continue the work necessary for healthy healing.

Obstacles

You may want to resist reaching out and asking for help. Avoid ignoring the recommendation to have a few people or family members you can call upon to talk with and assist you with caring for you and with the children, if applicable. This support in your life is a vital part of your healing. You must be able to share how you are feeling. You will need someone to be real and transparent so that you don't keep the emotions and pain bottled up inside. You don't want the pressure to get so high that you explode in ways that could be harmful and inappropriate.

Remember, a support group for individuals working through a divorce or a professional therapist are also options if you don't have friends or family you can call upon who can identify with what you are going through or be the nurturing support you need.

When you are feeling different emotions, you may be tempted to try to avoid them by ignoring what you feel. If you keep them locked inside, you can't process them and if you don't work through them you won't heal properly. Resist the urge to not do the work, push your way through the different emotions. It may be painful and exhausting, but it will be so worth the work in the end. Remember to do the journaling as you face your pain and differing emotions. Describe what you are feeling, try to identify why you feel a certain way, and write it down. If you have a solution for something you've been dealing with writing it down. Write, write, and write, whatever the thoughts or feelings, just write. When you are at a settling point, write how you want to feel, some positive emotion that you want like joy, serenity, or love. Then, write down some positive affirmations.

Forgiving someone is a difficult challenge. It can be even more challenging if you believe the person does not deserve your forgiveness. And forgiving yourself can be difficult. Think about the heavy load of ill feelings inside—

anger, bitterness, hate, and resentment—these emotions you are carrying around with you every day, they are you hurting you.

The tendency to ignore this portion (forgiving) of the healing can be tempting because you may feel they or you don't deserve to be forgiven. Ask yourself why, and let's add these feelings to the journal. If you are feeling stuck here, consider reaching out for some spiritual support or a professional therapist. Remember, forgiveness does not mean you have to be friends with someone. You don't even have to see or speak with the person again. Restoring interaction is not the point and neither is it the goal. Freedom from your past is the focus. The act of forgiving is a personal choice, and you have to first want to forgive to move forward. When dealing with abuse, you should reach out for professional support so that you can move cautiously through this.

You may get tired of the routine and not want to do this every day, but the repetition is what makes this work. Avoid the temptation to excuse yourself from the exercises in the, they're important to building up your self-image and confidence.

Our children are our most valuable treasures. Don't slip up and bring them into all the drama. Even if you are feeling lonely, avoid leaning on your children and venting to them about your ex and all the hurt you are feeling. The temptation may be strong to vent about all the bad things their dad has done or how he is hurting you or neglecting them. Don't do it. Don't paint a negative picture of their dad to them. Let them form their own opinions. You want them to be protected as much as possible from all the ugliness that can come with a divorce, and you want to give them a fair chance at believing in marriage when they're older and considering having a family.

Being too close to someone too soon can be a stumbling block to your healing. Move cautiously when thinking about dating. Getting involved too soon can pause your healing because you may want a mate to avoid grieving your ex, and you may end up in a rebound and wake up one day and say, "I don't like him." It's common for people to run to a new relationship to make themselves feel better. Be strong. Move slowly.

You may think carving out personal space to replenish yourself spiritually is not necessary. Even if you are not a Christian, taking time to de-stress and relax in solitude can be replenishing and is healthy emotionally and physically. With so much activity in our busy lives, you may find it hard to get away from the noise and focus on your spiritual growth and well-being. Spending time in prayer and reflecting on biblical teaching will strengthen you. Avoid the temptation to put nourishing your soul and spirit on the back burner. Make it a priority. It is so worth it.

When you are always helping others, it is easy to avoid doing what is good for you. Don't ignore yourself. Put you first. You deserve to feel good about yourself and to feel happy. Take the time necessary to do what is best for you. Don't let anything hold you back, girl. As my daughter would say, "Chop, chop, and get to it."

CHAPTER - 14
HOW TO LEARN TO LIVE AND LOVE AFTER BEING WITH A NARCISSIST

Mistakes to Avoid

Don't Believe That Knowledge Alone Will Keep You Safe. You bought this, you acquainted yourself thoroughly with the tactics and red flags that have let you know your partner, friend, or family member is indeed, a narcissist. That is only the first step, however. You had to implement new, unfamiliar, even unnatural behaviors just to regain some semblance of rationality so you could escape that narcissist, and therein lies the key to a successful recovery.

Now one of the most important things you have to do is continue the momentum you started by leaving (or deciding to leave, if you have not yet left). Persistence in action is what will deliver you from the heart of darkness, now and in the future. You have to keep going, keep pushing, keep trying, and never let your guard down. This is a lot to take, and a lot to handle. But it beats remaining in an environment designed to eventually kill you. No one can survive in a toxic environment forever.

Now that you know you must keep being active in your recovery, one of the most important things you'll need to understand is that your conscious mind does not have the tools it requires to heal your emotional, psychological damage that was caused by the narcissist. As a survivor, you have inner trauma that's going to have to be dealt with. Knowledge about narcissism, and even acknowledging what has happened won't repair the wounds deep within your heart. You're going to have to seek help for this, such as seeing a therapist well-versed in recovery from narcissistic abuse or join a support group. Any place where you can gain the wisdom of others who have gone before you will help you on the road to healing.

It would be relatively easy to look at the narcissist and see only the sadist, the manipulator, the cruel person who hurts others for fun. This point of view is not entirely accurate. The narcissist's problems run much deeper, and she is not hurting for fun, she's hurting other people because compared to non-narcissists, her reactions, observations, and perceptions of other people and herself are woefully fractured.

Never Leaving Your Place of Shame. Many of us will struggle to get past this step, especially those of us who once prided ourselves on being strong, tough, and self-reliant. Many men struggle deeply with being victims of narcissism; this is not something that's supposed to happen to them, right? Wrong. Narcissists target anyone who catches their interest, and they like to aim high. You were once capable of success, achievements, and love—and you will be, again, as soon as you get over blaming yourself for the abuse. You are not at fault—only the narcissist is.

Distraction, Instead of a Focal Shift. Further on we're going to talk about the need for a shift in focus while you recover. This is not the same as a constant distraction. Keeping yourself from thinking about what happened is only prolonging both the pain as well as the healing. You need to set aside some time on a regular basis to do some deep self-searching and work on tackling recovery, one step at a time.

Love on the Rebound. One of the most dangerous mistakes, replacing the missing "love," if it can be called that, with new love opens us to a particularly devious occurrence: meeting and becoming victim to yet another narcissist. At this stage in the game, you are not recovered, rebuilt, or reclaimed enough to be steady on your feet. You wouldn't be able to see the next abuser coming, even armed with the knowledge of what it takes to be a narcissist. You might accidentally (or on purpose) let slip about the abuse you suffered at the hands of your ex, and this could provide the new predator tons of ammunition in winning you over, sweeping you off your feet, then controlling your every move as both your savior and your new commander.

Additionally, you might have a lot of dark feelings after your traumatic experience—even if the new love is a genuine, well-meaning person, do you want to expose them to all the anger, resentment, and pain you've had to hide for so long? It's in there, even if you believe you've let it go. Only time and self-work can get it out, and so early on in your healing process is not the time to begin a new romance.

Don't Stalk the Narcissist. Of course, we don't do this because we want them back (usually), but because we're afraid. We want to keep up a perimeter of defenses and being pre-emptive and going on the offensive to see what the narcissist is up to seems perfectly natural, and it is. However, it also opens you up to contact. You must steadfastly adhere to the No Contact rule if you want to survive recovery and get your life back.

In addition, you might catch a glimpse of the person we call "The Replacement." The narcissist loathes being alone; she must have someone to feed her need for narcissistic supply or she will quickly self-destruct, so in your absence, she will find another victim. If you were to watch this play out on social media, you would be devastated and horrified to see that the exact process of "love-bombing," down to the places the narcissist goes with their new beau, to important proclamations of love and events they post about, almost exactly match yours when your relationship was in its inception. This can cause feelings of jealousy and hurt, even if we believe that we absolutely despise our former abuser. We might be tempted to reach out—perhaps tricking ourselves into believing that we are burying the hatchet. Even a simple message of "Congratulations, I'm so happy for you" can lead to terrible consequences.

Rebuilding Your Self

This may seem like an impossible task, or at least, a daunting one. How does one go about the business of rebuilding self? To start, you need to quickly and firmly establish boundaries.

Because you are reacquainting yourself with what it means to have boundaries, it's important to take things slowly with new friendships, and leave dating until you've healed much more.

Practice moments of boundary-enforcement during moments you're comfortable. If a social setting is too much for you right now, give yourself permission to opt out.

Reclaiming Your Reality

Forgive yourself and seek reminders of who you are. This is another time-consuming process, and should never be rushed. Don't allow so-called friends and family members guilt you into "getting over it"; this is especially true for men recovering from abuse. Take as much time as you need and tell those who would push too hard to take a hike. This is an important first step in recovering yourself. You were a strong, capable person once, and you will be again. The first thing you need to do is treat yourself with respect, and demand that others in your close circles do, too.

Seek out friends and family who were close to you during the good times before you met the narcissist. Ask them to help you; perhaps plan a trip to a place you had some good times or re-read articles or stories you wrote that garnered praise. Pull out old sports trophies and look through yearbooks and albums. You are on a mission to find you. You're out there somewhere, waiting to once again live happily. The narcissist never new you—they never even saw you. Don't be afraid to like yourself again;

it's necessary to achieve success and joy in life.

Redefining Your Belief System

Understand that a part of you knew that abuse was happening, and don't think less of yourself because of it. It's time to acknowledge the truth of what happened to you:

- You were tricked (because the other person is a narcissist).
- You were lied to (because the other person is a narcissist).
- You were manipulated (because the other person is a narcissist).
- You were hurt (because the other person is a narcissist).
- You were abused (because the other person is a narcissist).

The reason for the repetition is to help you get it into your head that there is only one reason these things happened, and that reason is listed above. You did not deserve to be hurt. You did nothing that warranted the abuse. You are simply not to blame.

Most people do not abuse others. There are so many people out there who would never dream of hurting you, who at the very least would show you a minimum of respect, and at the most would love you for the person you are, not the shadow they wish to torment. What you're doing now is strengthening yourself, so that you can once again believe that there's good in the world. Always remember, take this process one step at a time, and don't feel as if you're not making the process fast enough.

Rebuilding Your Trust

This part of the process may take the longest. This is a difficult part.

When dealing with people in your various friendships and acquaintances, give people the opportunity to show their intention. Call them on it. Ask them about their intentions. You can do this neutrally, even in a friendly tone—this is not a call to arms and you never need to sound combative. Being assertive and seeing with both eyes open is a healthy way of dealing with other people. Don't be afraid to take the initiative.

You're going to reach a point where you realize that part of you knew what was going on while you were with your abuser, and that's going to hurt. That will feel like a metric ton of shame, but you have to process it. All of us want to be happy; we want love, we want joy. You were holding out for that, but it never came. This is not your fault.

You're going to have to examine why you made the choices you did that brought you together with the narcissist—again, this is not blame. It's understanding yourself. Self-inquiry is one of the hardest but most important steps of the healing process. By learning about your vulnerabilities, you can learn how to better protect yourself in the future and learn how to forgive yourself because of the past.

Taking Steps towards Loving Again

Heal your inner child. Reclaim your joy. Look at relationships in a balanced, healthy way. What can I bring to the table? What am I asking of a new partner?

To start, you will need to shift your focus away from the concept of love for a while. This might seem counterintuitive, but you have a lot of rebuilding to do.

Finally, you are going to need a lot of patience. You will not be rebuilt in a day, just like that famous Italian city. You're healing and recovery will take time, as much time as it needs, and you are worth every minute it takes. You deserve to be happy and to be loved in a healthy, uplifting way.

CHAPTER - 15
TRANSFORMING YOUR FUTURE INTERACTIONS

Moving Forward

Handling an unhealthy/extreme narcissist is not an easy task, whether you choose to walk away or remain engaged in their lives to some degree. If you decide to walk away and cut contact, how you handle this move is an important consideration. For non-abusive narcissists, being empathetic and considerate ensures that you can walk away feeling positive about your actions. Remember, the narcissist is unable to empathize at times, and this is often due to increased emotional sensitivity. Letting them down gently without confrontation or exposing them may be the kindest route to prevent them from suffering a major blow to their self-esteem. However, in relationships where abuse is present, it may be advisable to cut the relationship swiftly, or in whatever way is safe and expedient for you.

When the Narcissist Returns—like any person involved in a relationship, it is likely that the narcissist will at some point think of you and contact you. Depending on your relationship and the individual, they may be very hurt, angry, or suspicious about why you are no longer involved with them. This may be understandably so. For example, if you decided to stop speaking to a parent because their actions were detrimental to your well-being- their parental love for you (whether hidden or clearly displayed) will not simply disappear. It is claimed by many that narcissists do not love, but this is rarely the case, and only applicable at the very upper limits of the scale. It is more likely that they are unable to express or show their love in the presence of other people. Many narcissists find that their loving feelings become apparent when they emerge temporarily from the grips of their addiction to narcissistic supply.

They may contact you in a caring, human manner, to gloat, or in a manipulative attempt to reel you back in and gain something they want from you. Each situation, like each individual, is different. When possible, in response to these contact attempts, empathy is advisable, but delivered in a way that does not invite hope, questions, or doubts. Be firm and stand by what you know is best, rather than being open to what they may offer you.

For example, if you have left a relationship with an emotionally abusive narcissist you may find that they contact you again in the future. Refusing contact is advisable, rather than discussing or reasoning with them, as no good can come from the interaction, only further harm. If they increase their attempts to contact you, become angry, emotional, or abusive, a strict attitude of no reaction can eventually force them to gain control of themselves, and move on. However, if you have been keeping your distance from a non-abusive family member—with unhealthy but not overwhelming narcissistic tendencies—you might welcome the opportunity to have a positive and well-meaning conversation. This does not mean that you are opening yourself up for dangerous or pre-emptive closeness but simply means that you are experimenting with being present in their lives, so long as they are able to behave in a reasonable manner. If they are still unable to behave well, then you may decide whether you want to continue the relationship or increase the distance further.

How to Change a Narcissist – Essentially, if someone is being unhealthily narcissistic, it is up to them to notice and correct their behavior, rather than anyone else to point it out to them and risk the backlash from a narcissistic injury. Healthy narcissism may work well, but it is important that it does not develop into dependence on approval and attention to an extreme degree in the long run. Highly narcissistic people are usually unaware that they are so, as they live very often in a state of denial and are unlikely to attempt to improve or work on themselves. In some cases, suspecting or being diagnosed with having NPD can provide significant motivation for people to change, as was found by Dr. Craig Malkin of Harvard medical school. During online discussions on identifying narcissism, he found the most distressed and heartfelt pleas for help and advice on how to improve came not from people in the lives of narcissists, but from those that had been diagnosed with or suspected they had NPD.

Happily, he believes that narcissists are able to change the ways in which they see the world, but that this rarely happens. This is because, in the case of narcissists, many will live, perpetually unaware or in denial of their skewed lens, and will never attempt to improve it. Although we cannot condemn those that want to change with a sentence of "irrevocably permanent narcissism"—for change to happen a person has to want to change and be capable of facing the work necessary to make improvements. It is no one else's responsibility to make this happen but the person who is overly narcissistic themselves.

This means that if you are caught up in the life of a narcissist, whether you decide to make them aware of your suspicions or not, nothing can make them improve unless they decide that they are ready to do so. This decision may come at a point of desperation, and real progress- if it comes at all- may take many years to solidify.

To overcome narcissism, the first step is to recognize the role of addiction to narcissistic supply and stop attempting to secure it. Accepting that being ordinary is okay is essential, and that no matter what successes or failures life brings—a person can never become more than just a person- equal to everyone else. The urge to stand out from to overcome narcissism, the first step is to recognize the role of addiction to narcissistic supply and stop attempting to secure it. Accepting that being ordinary is okay is essential, and that no matter what successes or failures life brings- a person can never become more than just a person- equal to everyone else. The urge to stand out from the crowd needs to be quashed.

If it's impossible to stop supplying the ego— then aligning this need with a positive cause can at least make a difference in the world. Like any addiction, fighting it can be extremely difficult, and overcoming it whilst still being intoxicated is highly unlikely to happen. Rather than fighting to remain in control of narcissism, the narcissist must take responsibility for starving it and going "cold turkey," as with any alcoholic or drug addict.

Assessing the Situation Objectively – you may be fully aware that you are a source of narcissistic supply, a target for manipulation, or abusive behavior. Perhaps it is clear that you must either break off or continue the relationship. But for those who are still in the questioning phase, unsure about what is happening and the extent to which they need to act, there are several exercises you can do to help you see more clearly. Extreme narcissistic people may be abusive if they are unhealthy enough, as they may be unable to be empathetic to others. If you're unsure as to whether you're involved in an abusive interaction, take a look at the following checklist. Many victims of abuse live in a state of denial regarding the true nature of the situation, making justifications for their loved ones and excusing their abusive behavior. Abuse can be an insidious process that can leave the victim feeling confused and upset for an extended period after it has finished. It can have crippling effects on the victim's sense of self-worth and confidence and should not be ignored or allowed to continue after it has been identified.

There are various types of abuse – emotional/psychological, sexual, physical, and financial/material. As a summary, you have the right to emotional support in your relationships, be heard by your partner, and be responded to with courtesy. You also have the right to have your feelings and experiences acknowledged as real and valid, clear, and informative answers to questions that concern you, to live free from criticism and judgment, live free from accusation and blame. You should receive encouragement, live free from emotional and physical threats and be respectfully asked to do things rather than "ordered." You should receive goodwill from your partner and live free from angry outbursts and rage. Each type of abuse has various indicators split out in the lists below. If you're unsure about whether you are experiencing abuse, identify which indicators apply to your relationship with the person in question. Multiple indicators mean that it is more likely that what you are experiencing classifies as abuse.

CONCLUSION

I commend you for reading through this. You invested in yourself. You made a commitment and kept it. I hope your heart has been stirred and your soul inspired. You have been given the gift of tools you can apply to rebuild your life. You have received encouragement and you've read stories of other women just like yourself. I'd like to reach out to you across space and time to give you a hug and to look into your eyes. I'd like to say to you, "You are amazing. You have a good heart and you are worthy of following your dreams. You have so much to give, and there is no one on this Earth who has the life experience, knowledge, and unique gifts that you possess. You matter, and you can rebuild your life to one of joy and purpose, and you can truly make a difference for others. This is your time to re-create yourself into the fullness of your being that has been suppressed for so long."

I wrote much of this either sitting in my sunny bay window in my kitchen, or in my motorhome parked by the water. Each time I sat down to write and pour out my soul to you, I breathed deeply, dropped into my heart, and infused my message with love. This is my love letter to the women who have been hurt, let down, betrayed, disappointed, humiliated, and led to believe they are somehow unlovable and unworthy. You are beautiful! You have so much to give. When you release your fear, you will be filled with joy and hope. Fear is the opposite of love. Make the choice to live your life in love. Lead with your heart. Discover your message, and then share it, to inspire others to live their lives being all they're meant to be.

Now is the time for your new beginning. Anything you've ever longed for wished you could do, fantasized that perhaps "one day" you could achieve, can now be yours. I know that is a bold statement. I'll venture a guess that you read that and thought something like, "Me? I don't have the money, or the talent, or the skills. I'm too old. I'm past my prime. It's just too late for me." I assure you, it is never too late! Your life will not become grand overnight, but if you work through this, seek support, learn to love yourself, feed your soul, face your fears, and refuse to give up, you will rebuild your life and you will be happy. You will live a life of meaning and purpose.

Will you resign yourself to the alternative? Will you stay stuck, miserable, and unfulfilled? It is up to you, but you certainly do not have to settle for a directionless and small life. I pour my heart into my work with women because I truly believe women are powerful and amazing beyond words, and they deserve to live spectacular lives. We have been given false messages about our weaknesses, inadequacies, and imperfections. It's time to stand together in strength and celebration! We deserve happiness and fulfillment!

Move forward, in the direction of your dreams every day, even if it's in small increments. Surround yourself with people who support and inspire you. Keep the momentum going? Utilize the tools you've been given. Nurture yourself, on a daily basis. When you have decisions to make, breathe deeply, drop into your heart, and ask for guidance. Then follow your instincts and go forward. You are on a healing journey. You have life lessons to learn. You have great wisdom to draw from. You are in this life to contribute to the unique gifts and talents you've developed. What will your legacy be? What great things will you accomplish?

How do you feel now?

Do you feel well informed and confident that you're clear on the road ahead? Do you feel like you might be ready to take the first step towards initiating divorce proceedings? Have the contents of the book helped you to understand that none of this is your fault and that you're free to walk away?

We hope that you feel more positive at this stage. Whilst it's normal to feel sad at the same time because you're about to end a marriage that you hoped would last you a lifetime, it's important to realize that you do not deserve to live your life in the grips of a narcissist and their constant manipulation and control.

You can set yourself free, and whilst the road ahead may not be smooth, it will come to an end and leave you with a brighter future ahead.

Divorce of any kind is messy and difficult. Choosing your divorce attorney carefully is vital. As we've mentioned several times throughout the book, choosing an attorney who has specific experience and deep knowledge of narcissism is important. In this case, they can help you to navigate everything that the narcissist may throw your way and help you to end the divorce with a fair result.

HEALING AFTER A DIVORCE FROM A NARCISSIST

If you have children, remember that they must always come first. We obviously don't have to tell you this, but it's a point that's worth making. When a divorce takes hold, things can become overwhelming and when you add narcissism to the mix, it's even easier for the whole situation to turn very sour indeed.

Stay as positive as you can be, focus on the future, understand that whilst the road ahead may not be easy, it will be worthwhile in the end. Choose your attorney carefully, be sure of what you want, plan everything out, and seek support from those close to you. If you have to mend some broken bridges in order to build up your support network, don't be afraid to do so.

Life does not have to be controlled by a narcissist. You do not have to be manipulated and you do not have to live your life trying to please someone who will never be pleased.

Look to the future with hope and happiness will come your way.

Believe in yourself. I believe in you. You've got this!

www.ingramcontent.com/pod-product-compliance
Lightning Source LLC
Chambersburg PA
CBHW070053120526
44588CB00033B/1417